UNSTUCK

UNSTUCK

How the Savior Frees Us
from Our Favorite Sins

ROBERT REYNOLDS

DESERET
BOOK

Library of Congress Cataloging-in-Publication Data

Reynolds, Robert, 1974–   author.
    Unstuck : how the Savior frees us from our favorite sins / Robert Reynolds.
        pages cm
    Includes bibliographical references and index.
    ISBN 978-1-62972-115-6 (paperbound)
1. Atonement—The Church of Jesus Christ of Latter-day Saints. 2. Repentance—The Church of Jesus Christ of Latter-day Saints. 3. Forgiveness of sin. I. Title. II. Title: How the Savior frees us from our favorite sins.
    BX8643.A85R49 2015
    248.4'89332—dc23   2015028994

Printed in the United States of America
Publishers Printing, Salt Lake City, UT

10   9   8   7   6   5   4   3   2   1

CONTENTS

INTRODUCTION

This book was not written by a General Authority. In fact, it was written by a sinner. I'm not joking; it's true. Are you going to keep reading?

Does it help to know that it was written by a reluctant sinner? A faithful sinner who is trying to improve? If you're feeling some hesitation, I understand. Who am I to write a Church book? I'm not a stake president, BYU professor, or even a seminary teacher. But then, they are all sinners too.

I manage rock bands—that's what I do. That and entertainment law. My office is on Las Vegas Boulevard, two doors down from a strip club. I walk past barely dressed go-go dancers on poker tables on my way to hotel dinners and then work late hours in a recording studio. Or I go on tour with a rock band. I walk around festival grounds and come home smelling like Amsterdam.

Yet I do have this going for me: I know about temptation. I understand the allure—how it coaxes you in and slowly ties you up. I am immersed in a business and city obsessed with making sin seductive. And, if you and I were in the same room, perhaps I might look down and whisper how, at times, I've fallen prey.

But maybe that's useful to admit even here, because I know a secret: you're a sinner too. You don't have to say it out loud. We both know I'm right. Despite my unconventional résumé for a "Church book" author, you should read this because you can relate.

Even the most righteous Latter-day Saints do more than

"make mistakes" (we love that euphemism, don't we?). We deliberately sin. The Bible and Book of Mormon proclaim that "all have sinned, and come short of the glory of God" (Romans 3:23) and that "all we, like sheep, have gone astray" (Mosiah 14:6). Without exception—our parents, spouses, bishops, stake presidents, you name it—every one of us is a repeating spiritual lawbreaker.[1] Yet too often we feel alone. Ashamed of our weaknesses, we hide behind masks of false perfection. And, frankly, that doesn't help anyone.

Full of shame and loneliness, too many of us believe our imperfections are particularly damning and that our ability to overcome those imperfections is uniquely weak. Perhaps if we overcame each sin right when it occurred we would more readily admit our struggles. We could share inspiring stories of defeating weaknesses swiftly and surely. Unfortunately, the battle with sin rarely works that way.

It seems that very few Latter-day Saints explore the entire spectrum of transgression. Instead, we have certain disobedient behaviors that, for one reason or another, we do not permanently stop. We sin and repent, sin and repent, repeatedly going through the same thoughts and the same actions. This pattern also applies to sins of omission. Just like addictive sins of commission, sins of omission—not doing what you know you should—can become habits unaligned with the will of God.

This pattern is not just frustrating; it jeopardizes our salvation. In fact, when we fall back into the same sinful behavior time and time again, we miss out on true repentance, which is "essential to our temporal and eternal happiness."[2] True repentance requires that we "forsake" our sins permanently (D&C 58:43). This book is written for all people who find themselves in this damning rut (everyone, perhaps?).

So, let's be real: temptations are tempting. At times, it can feel nearly impossible to overcome them. On a personal note, I have often wanted to change a specific behavior (or so I thought), but despite my good intentions, I have repeatedly tripped and fallen over the same hurdles. This has left me frustrated enough to wonder whether I even had the ability to do otherwise.

This cycle is difficult to reconcile. I had a testimony; I knew a behavior was wrong; I did not want to repeat it (right?). Yet I repeated it, nonetheless. Even going to the Savior and asking Him to help me change began to feel insincere. "You can't change. Why try?" asked the devil. This awful question was awfully persuasive.

But the devil is wrong. We can change; we just cannot do it alone.

Unfortunately, even in church—the one place we should experience less shame and loneliness and more empowering strength—too many of us feel more shameful, more uniquely weak, and more alone. This should never happen.

We are not a church of sinless people. Regardless of our white shirts and ties, we all stray from what we know is right, repent sincerely—or often halfheartedly—and then later commit those same sins. Our actions show that the previous round of repentance "didn't take." The church is not a museum for the perfect, as they say, but a hospital for the sick,[3] and each one of us is perpetually unwell.

I wish there were a formal way for us to stand up and admit our struggles, like alcoholics at an AA meeting. Even that mighty prophet Nephi confessed: "My heart exclaimeth: O wretched man that I am! Yea, my heart sorroweth because of my flesh; my soul grieveth because of mine iniquities. I am encompassed about, because of the temptations and the sins which do so easily beset me.

And when I desire to rejoice, my heart groaneth because of my sins" (2 Nephi 4:17–19).

Incidentally, the fact that we are all "easily beset" by temptations and sin is not an excuse. Recognizing we are not alone could be used to rationalize failure, but it shouldn't; it ought to give us strength. People sin. But people also overcome their sins. Every day, men and women who were once bound by seemingly never-ending sinful behavior make permanent change.

However—this is essential—we must recognize that overcoming habitual sin takes more than sheer will. Although by ourselves we often feel helpless, there is a way to overcome every personal rut, to become "unstuck" from every cycle of sin. When Satan tells you after years of struggling with a repeated sin that you can't change, he is—as with all of his greatest lies—partially correct. You, alone, cannot change. Your heart is damaged. Yet despite how hard your heart has become, our Heavenly Father can "take away the stony heart" and give unto you a "heart of flesh" (Ezekiel 36:26). He can even remove a particular temptation such that we "have no more disposition to do evil, but to do good continually" (Mosiah 5:2). In fact, our very weaknesses can become their diametrically opposed strengths! To the frustrated, repeating sinner, this news is fantastic. It is so fantastic as to border on unbelievable.

We all need this. To experience a new birth "of the Spirit" and "become new creatures," qualified to inherit our Father's kingdom, we must each receive a mighty change of heart at least once in our lifetime (Mosiah 27:24, 26).[4] Lesser changes of heart also are needed for every cycle of sin in which we find ourselves.

Once we are granted a mighty change of heart—when our disposition toward sin and receptiveness to the Spirit are as they should be—we need to implement scriptural principles to maintain the exceeding joy, perfect peace, and love that only He can give.

If there is one principle here that stands out, it is the need for good old-fashioned "wanting it." Christ and prophets throughout the ages have proclaimed that in the end, our loving Father will grant us what we sincerely, humbly desire. We can have mighty changes in our hearts and dispositions. Each one of us. This is mandatory and attainable. We just need to want it.

PART ONE

SIN AND WEAKNESS

CHAPTER 1

WHY DO WE REPEATEDLY COMMIT THE SAME SINS?

*And there shall also be many which shall say: Eat, drink,
and be merry; nevertheless, fear God—he will justify in
committing a little sin; yea, lie a little, take the advantage
of one because of his words, dig a pit for thy neighbor;
there is no harm in this; and do all these things, for
tomorrow we die; and if it so be that we are guilty,
God will beat us with a few stripes, and at last
we shall be saved in the kingdom of God.*

2 NEPHI 28:8

When I was a new missionary in South Carolina, a member shared a secret he had learned after serving fourteen years as bishop: *"We all narrow our sins down to the few we enjoy."*

This bothered me. Did believing Latter-day Saints honestly *enjoy* certain sins and choose to repeat them regardless of their consequences? Why? Could I, or anyone, enjoy a life of repeated sin? Didn't Alma tell his son that "wickedness never was happiness" (Alma 41:10)? Prophets say this all the time. If they're right, then why do we repeatedly commit the same sins that keep us from eternal happiness and—more to the point—don't even make us happy in *this* life?!

Before addressing why we sin, let's clarify what sin actually is. Ignorantly acting contrary to a commandment may constitute transgression, but it is not necessarily sin. The half brother of Jesus taught, "To him that knoweth to do good, and doeth it not, to him it is sin" (James 4:17). Note sin's subjective nature: when anyone acts contrary to his or her personal knowledge of God's will, "*to him* it is sin." Moreover, the "things of God" can only be "spiritually discerned" (1 Corinthians 2:11, 14).

> We all narrow our sins down to the few we enjoy.

So, in order for us to sin, we need to first receive personal confirmation—by the Holy Spirit or light of Christ[5]—that what we are doing (or not doing) is wrong. Yet, even when we do receive this spiritual confirmation, we still sin repeatedly. Why? This is a fundamental question. Here is the answer: *At first we sin because we think we want to—eventually we sin because we literally cannot help ourselves.*

At First, We Sin Because We Think We Want To

This point is so universal that we can begin with a story from your life. Yes, you. Odds are, this is a true story. When you were around fifteen, you were curious about something that your parents or Church leaders said you should avoid. You didn't want to sin, per se. You didn't specifically plan on doing anything wrong. You were just an innocent kid with an inquiring mind. And, to your fifteen-year-old self, eager for new experiences, a certain activity seemed intriguing. *What will this feel like? What will happen if I try this?* you might have thought. The curiosity kept coming to your mind. So, one small step at a time, you found out. At first, it probably all felt so innocent, so natural.

Perhaps most sins begin with innocuous intentions. Many first encounters start off as seemingly harmless desires to experience something new. Countless people have developed addictions to pornography, for example, as a result of little more than biologically driven curiosity.[6] There are few alcoholic drinks that I, as a food and beverage lover, haven't been at least curious to try. After all, I've eaten snails, tongue tacos, rattlesnake meat, ants, and fried scorpions just to see what they taste like.

Following the pursuit of something new, we are often over-confident in our ability to fight temptation. We get too close. President Harold B. Lee compared this to butterflies and a flame. "Many of these beautiful human butterflies winged for heavenly flight have fallen with wings singed and badly seared," he wrote, "because of their curiosity about the forbidden."[7] Too often, curiosity is the Trojan horse that introduces seemingly innocent behaviors that later become addictive and destructive.

Other times, sin begins with motivations like carelessness or indifference. The chance to sin arises and, with little thought, we merely let it happen. We can all remember instances like this. Maybe a friend teased another girl in school and you smiled and walked away. The awkward kid wanted a seat at your table or in your study group, and you didn't make room. Your boss had the wrong impression of what you did, but because that impression was favorable, you didn't bother to correct her.

> At first we sin because we think we want to— eventually we sin because we literally cannot help ourselves.

In short, whether from curiosity or carelessness, we never "mean" to do something wrong (or so we say). It just happens.

Or perhaps we sometimes know we are heading down a path we shouldn't travel, but fleeting pleasures along the way are too tempting. "I'll try this just a little bit longer," we tell ourselves. From minor prescription pill abuse to eventual rehab or from white lies to perjury and prison, increasingly damaging sins come as easily as placing one foot in front of the other—while facing the wrong direction.

Seemingly benign motivations are wolves in sheep's clothing. There is no acceptable excuse to knowingly act against the will of God. And there are always real consequences.

Many have compelling rationalizations for misbehavior. I once spent four months volunteering in a classroom full of second-graders born addicted to cocaine. I remember a little girl who couldn't concentrate enough to count a handful of paper clips and a restless, filthy boy who had no food besides what he got in school. Drug addiction was only one of the bad cards they were dealt.

Some children are affected by molestation or other types of abuse. These wounds have lasting effects. As Elder Dallin H. Oaks noted, the "victims of physical and sexual and emotional abuse are more susceptible to Satan's manipulations. They are more likely to perpetuate these ugly transgressions within their own family relationships."[8]

Even those who seem most fortunate have their own spiritual handicaps. We are born into a flawed world with imperfect bodies, imperfect parents, imperfect teachers (even Church leaders), and a culture where the pursuit of instant pleasure reigns supreme. These circumstances certainly do affect us and, at times, even seem like excuses for sinful behavior.

Have no doubt: this is a world where we can indeed be "acted upon," whether by false teachers, the media, bad influences, or temptations of the natural world and our own natural inclinations (see Mosiah 3:19). However, as Lehi's final words proclaim, ultimately we make the choice "to act for [our]selves" or "to be acted upon" (2 Nephi 2:26). We are all "free to choose liberty . . .

or to choose captivity" and cannot abdicate that responsibility (2 Nephi 2:27).

We need to admit that at some point prior to committing a sin, we didn't only understand the commandment intellectually. Instead, the Spirit (or light of Christ) testified to us of God's will. And for whatever reason, we rejected His direction. *We sinned because we wanted to.*

This is how it starts.

Placing Our Will before God's Is Pride, the Great Vice

Our ability to rationalize starts young. Take, for example, a recent conversation between our five-year-old son, Max, and his mother.

Max: *Mom, I have a good brain.*

Erica: *Yes, Max, you do.*

Max: *Do you know why I like my brain? My brain tells me, "I won't rot if you play video games."*

Granted, it is possible that Max's brain is resilient to incessant video games. But I doubt it. Regardless of what his brain did or didn't say, the point is that *Max believes this because he wants to.*

Two thousand years ago, Korihor also led people astray with false doctrines that were "pleasing unto the carnal mind" (Alma 30:53). In fact, Korihor had so much success sharing false doctrine that he "withstood the truth" and believed the lies himself.

We are all inclined to take the pleasure-laden path. Doing what "comes naturally" is our biological instinct. And rationalizations become the songs we sing and stories we tell ourselves on that pleasant downhill journey. The entertainment industry is full of musicians, songwriters, actors, and filmmakers who have perfected the art of making short-term pleasure feel right. Most of us can admit it: those songs are on our playlists; those movies are in our DVRs.

We are each capable of the most imaginative rationalizations when it comes to "call[ing] evil good, and good evil" (2 Nephi 15:20). But when we receive spiritual confirmation that our acts oppose the will of God and then decide to *continue* committing those acts, we are committing the "universal sin, the great vice."[9]

In fact, the decision to choose our will over God's is the precursor to all repetitive sin: pride. President Ezra Taft Benson taught, "The proud cannot accept the authority of God giving direction to their lives. They pit their perceptions of truth against God's great knowledge, their abilities versus God's priesthood power, their accomplishments against His mighty works."[10] This tendency has been around forever.

Remember, once the Nephites became prosperous, they no longer wanted to keep commandments or have God as "their guide" (Helaman 12:6). The Lord compelled them to be humble, they repented, and they again received His blessings. Then, finding themselves prosperous and blessed again, they once more became prideful and increasingly sinful. Like we all learned in Sunday School, this "pride cycle" reoccurred until the "pride of . . . the Nephites, ha[d] proven their destruction" (Moroni 8:27).

Referring to this message "written for our day,"[11] modern revelation warns, "Beware of pride, lest ye become as the Nephites of old" (D&C 38:39). We must not allow our lives to become so comfortable and self-centered that we avoid being "bothered" by the Lord or frustrated by His rules and regulations.

Like Max and his video games, we too often think we know best how we'd like to spend our Sunday afternoon, how we ought to spend our money, what we should or shouldn't consume, or what we ought to see. We innately flex our agency and resist being told what to do. And as a result, we pit our will against more than just God's will. We end up unwittingly making choices that are *against our own best interest,* against our lasting peace and joy—even our eternal salvation.

Pride's role is evident not only when we act upon our weaknesses. Pride connected with our strengths can lead to sin as well. Elder Dallin H. Oaks gave numerous examples of this, including exploiting spiritual gifts for our own ego, focusing our studies on obscure doctrines and history at the exclusion of faith and fundamentals, sacrificing more than is appropriate, overzealous social consciousness, being overly focused on goals and losing balance in life, distortion of family duties, excessive giving, materialistic self-reliance, misapplying principles of love and tolerance, and even performing inordinate Church service.[12] In other words, when pride enters the picture, even our strengths can lead to repetitive sin.

"How, then, do we prevent our strengths from becoming our downfall?" asked Elder Oaks. "The quality we must cultivate is humility. Humility is the great protector. Humility is the antidote against pride."[13] God knows the course that leads to our greatest happiness. We just need to set our pride aside and follow Him.

Ultimately, We Sin—Even When We *Don't* Want to—Because We Literally Cannot Help Ourselves

I can't change, I can't change, I can't change, I can't change . . .
—"Bittersweet Symphony," by The Verve

I have another Max story. The other day, Max asked, "What was heaven like? I don't know. I can't remember. All I can remember are orange paintings."

There is much we don't know about our premortal existence (including whether there were orange paintings). One thing we do know, however, is that we fought Satan and one-third of our spiritual siblings for the right to experience life on Earth with moral agency (see Moses 4:3; D&C 29:36). Ironically, now that we are here, many of us voluntarily give that up.

It's strange to think that we can lose our agency. But *lose* isn't the best word; *lose* suggests that we somehow involuntarily misplaced it. Instead, when we harden our hearts and pit our will against God's, we voluntarily use our agency to restrict the very freedom we want. As Lehi explained, we don't merely find ourselves captive—we actually "*choose captivity*" (2 Nephi 2:27; emphasis added).

That sounds crazy. Why would anyone choose captivity? Here's why: we don't realize what is happening until it is too late. In the moment, we don't notice that our agency is becoming compromised. We think we are simply traveling where we choose. Ironically, line upon line, rebellious acts of apparent freedom become the path to our enslavement.

As Nephi explained, Satan "leadeth [us] by the neck with a flaxen cord, until he bindeth [us] with his strong cords forever" (2 Nephi 26:22). Flax has soft, thin fibers that are easily broken. A single flaxen cord around the neck is virtually weightless. In other words, you don't feel it. But when we rationalize that initially imperceptible cord wrapping around us, and we don't break each flaxen cord through continual repentance, we ultimately find ourselves led by Satan and bound tighter than we are able to break.

The reason we do not recognize this progressive captivity—let alone try to escape—is because our hearts grow so hard over time that we ultimately become "past feeling" (Ephesians 4:19; 1 Nephi 17:45). This is a frightening concept.

Repeating a Sin Instead of Forsaking It Hardens Your Heart and Leads to Becoming "Past Feeling"

While attending New York University, I joined a group of sociology students that mentored juvenile felons. Each of us was assigned one kid who had spent at least a year in prison before the age of eighteen. My mentee (let's call him Anton) had recently left Rikers Island. Along with drug-related crimes, Anton was sentenced for murdering a rival gang member. Though on probation, he was still a "tribe leader" over one of the largest groups of Latin Kings in the New York area.

Every Tuesday night, Anton and I (along with the others) worked on anger management, career planning, and miscellaneous social skills. We ate pizza and one time went skiing. Over time, I got to know Anton well. I loved him, but I was also afraid of him. He reminded me of a serial killer.

> When we don't want the Spirit to interrupt our self-determined life of ease, our hearts slowly harden.

Anton had no remorse for killing that rival gangster. He once said he would shoot or stab anyone who stood between him and money. He didn't feel the slightest guilt over dealing drugs, and he felt no compassion over those lives left in his wake.

After an exercise in networking one night, Anton told me he was meeting a fellow gang member who wanted out. Anton said he was going to cut off either the tip of this kid's tongue or his little finger. I was horrified. Anton explained that those acts were symbolic, suggesting that if the gang member left the Latin Kings, he would never speak ill of or raise a finger against them. I tried to persuade Anton that if someone wanted to leave that dangerous life, he should let the person go.

Instead of feeling empathy, however, Anton was furious. He leapt to his feet and pressed me against the wall. Shouting, he refused to hear that his behavior was morally wrong. Like any psychopath, Anton had a heart impervious to compassion. You could say he had a hard heart. You could say his heart was so hard, in fact, that it had become past feeling.

On a lesser level, this happens to us all. It's easy to get defensive when someone points out our moral weaknesses. Likewise, each of us can become past feeling and hard-hearted. But how can this happen?

Happiness and success are often equated with access to creature comforts. We want comfortable shoes, comfortable beds, comfortable couches, and comfortable lives. As a popular marketing slogan suggests, we want "whatever's comfortable." And the more prosperity and success we experience, the less tolerance we have for discomfort.

But remorse and godly sorrow are not comfortable. So, as we do with any discomfort, we flinch when the Spirit pricks us. "Back off," we say. "I've got this. I've been doing just fine myself and would rather not be bothered." And the Holy Spirit— described as "the ultimate example of politeness"[14]—does exactly what we ask. He leaves us alone. And when He leaves, our hearts begin to harden.

Scriptures describe hard hearts as the condition of decreased receptiveness to the "still small voice" of the Holy Spirit (1 Kings 19:12). *When we don't want the Spirit to interrupt our self-determined life of ease, our hearts slowly harden.* It's like a callus on your foot. When your shoes are too tight, an area of skin becomes thick and hard in response to the repeated irritation. Your heart is no different. We don't want the Spirit to "keep bugging us," so unless we choose to repent (i.e., change that ill-fitting shoe), our hearts invariably harden.

The Nephites revealed this pattern before their destruction: "Yea, and we may see *at the very time when he doth prosper his people, . . .* doing all things for the welfare and happiness of his people; yea, *then is the time that they do harden their hearts,* and do forget the Lord their God, and do trample under their feet the Holy One—yea, and this *because of their ease, and their exceedingly great prosperity* (Helaman 12:2; emphasis added).[15]

Two thousand years later, we are just the same. "Because of our ease," we don't want a broken heart. So to protect our hearts from guilt and to keep feeling comfortable, we harden them. Perhaps this is why some say the gospel is "to comfort the afflicted and to afflict the [comfortable]."[16]

The Effects of Hard-Heartedness

So here's the answer to that question about whether we truly enjoy sins, sparked by a South Carolina bishop: *a hard heart allows us to mistakenly think we want to sin.* When our heart is not damaged, we don't want to sin. Alma was right. Wickedness never was happiness. As Moroni explained, it is not happiness but despair that comes from iniquity (see Moroni 10:22). "Please do not mistake the laughter of the world for genuine happiness," said Elder Neal A. Maxwell. "The laughter of the world is merely garrulous guilt trying to reassure itself. It is the sound of selfishness emanating from the cul-de-sac of terrible loneliness. Don't mistake it for something else."[17]

I am certain that no repetitive sin brings lasting peace or joy and that God's love vastly outweighs every shot of dopamine and fleeting pleasure. If our hearts were not damaged, we would never "narrow our sins down to the few we enjoy," because uncompromised hearts detest sin.

Only when we are past feeling do we continue making such poor decisions. This is similar to something I experienced as a young Scout. Camping in the snow, I had the poor judgment that accompanies being "past feeling." On two different occasions, I've warmed my frozen feet so close to a campfire that my shoes' rubber soles melted or the laces caught on fire. As many young Scouts learn, when your feet lose feeling, your judgment regarding how close you can safely get to fire is unreliable. Likewise, when your heart is insensitive to the Spirit's subtle promptings, you won't be able to discern the choices you will regret from the ones that lead to peace and joy. When we are cut off from the eternal foresight of our loving Heavenly Father, we all lack the capacity to decide in our ultimate best interest.

In fact, *hard hearts may be the pivotal difference between those who do and those who do not finally enter God's presence.* In the Joseph Smith Translation of the Bible, we read, "If they harden their hearts they shall not enter into my rest; also, I have sworn, If they will not harden their hearts, they shall enter into my rest" (Joseph Smith Translation, Hebrews 4:3). It all comes down to this.

Ultimately, We Can Lose Our Ability to Change

The consequences of repetitive sin and a hardened heart are even graver than becoming past feeling. It is one thing to no longer feel the Spirit warn you of the devil's ever-binding cords; it is quite another to become inescapably bound.

For clarity, this bondage is not always physiological addiction or compulsion. Any negative behavior—any sin of commission or omission—can become a continual and repetitive problem that you cannot seem to overcome.

Elder James E. Talmage taught that *the mere act of procrastinating repentance can lead to an inability to change.* "Repentance is not always [p]ossible," he wrote. "As the time of repentance is procrastinated, the ability to repent grows weaker; neglect of opportunity in holy things develops inability."[18]

From homework to chores, we all procrastinate what we find uncomfortable. We procrastinate even more when the deadline isn't pressing. *What deadline is less pressing in your life than its eventual end?* Therefore, we must remind ourselves that even if we live another fifty years, that moment when Satan's flaxen cord has us inescapably bound might be tomorrow.

> The mere act of procrastinating repentance can lead to an inability to change.

Whether we choose to continue in our personal cycle of sin due to pride and a hard heart or from shame in asking God to forgive us yet again, those flaxen cords will restrain us until we are overcome. And when the father of lies[19] tells us we cannot repent and make that definitive change, for once he may be telling the truth.

KEY POINTS

WHY DO WE SIN?

1. At first, we often sin for seemingly innocent motivations, such as curiosity or indifference.

2. Sometimes we sin by succumbing to temptations that offer short-term pleasure without concern for long-term peace or joy.

3. Regardless of the reason, we ultimately sin because (we think) we want to.

4. Choosing to sin instead of following God's will is a symptom of pride.

5. We don't want to feel guilty for making sinful choices that we know are wrong. The pangs of the Holy Spirit are uncomfortable and incompatible with a life of ease. We often try to avoid that irritation, and as a result, our hearts begin to harden.

6. With hard hearts and repentance procrastinated, we ultimately become "past feeling"—we lose our ability to overcome certain temptations and become captive by Satan's flaxen cords.

CHAPTER 2

GOD CAN MAKE ANY WEAKNESS A STRENGTH

We will not become perfect in a day or a month or
a year. We will not accomplish it in a lifetime, but we can
begin now, starting with our more obvious weaknesses
and gradually converting them to strengths
as we go forward with our lives.

GORDON B. HINCKLEY[20]

Too often, this is the record of our lives: side A—innocent encounters with temptation; side B—inescapable, repetitive sin.
We allow ourselves to try a little sin, our hearts grow hard, and
before we realize it, we become ensnared. Whether it's through
addictions to pornography or pain pills, extramarital flirtation, or
an out-of-control temper, getting trapped happens to the best of
us. Every single one of us has customized snares from which we
cannot seem to escape.

We all repeat patterns of behavior that we know are wrong.
We know they don't bring peace or joy. We are ashamed; sometimes we hide. Too often, we give up even trying to repent. It can
feel downright hopeless.

But hopelessness has no place in this gospel. From the Greek,
the word *gospel* means "good news." There is good news for every
slave to repetitive sin: *God works miracles.* God doesn't just calm
our pangs of hunger; He sends manna from heaven. He works
miracles beyond our comprehension. He is our loving Father who

always wants to help us in our time of need. Why do we forget this?

President Benson explained: "No one is more anxious to see us change our lives than the Father and the Savior. In the book of Revelation is a powerful and profound invitation from the Savior. He says, 'I stand at the door, and knock: if any man hear my voice, and open the door, I will come in to him' (Rev. 3:20). Note that He does not say, 'I stand at the door and wait for you to knock.' He is calling, beckoning, asking that we simply open our hearts and let Him in."[21]

He doesn't listen only when we call. *He* calls; we just need to listen. Our loving Father knows when, with restrained agency, we find ourselves in cycles of inescapable sin. No surgeon or therapist can cure the damage of a hardened heart. But our Heavenly Father can. He wants to. God can also ensure we benefit from trials—even those caused by our own mistakes—and turn our weaknesses into strengths.

Trials and Affliction Can Be for Our Gain

There is great news for the repentant sinner: all that heartache and pain we experienced, all those years of frustration over our weakness, do not have to be in vain! While we obviously don't want to make our lives any more difficult than necessary—that is, choosing sin is not the ideal way to grow—we were supposed to experience trials in this life.

In the premortal existence, we knew we would face trials on earth, and we knew that each one of us was going to make mistakes. This is a fallen state; of course we were going to fall. As Brad Wilcox said, "For a child learning to walk, falling down may not be desirable, but the lessons learned from it are."[22] Sin and its consequences have always been inevitable. Like Helaman's stripling warriors, we chose to face a battlefield where, even if we prevailed, not one of us would survive without having first "received many wounds" (Alma 57:25). And that's okay. Trials—even the painful consequences of our own repetitive sins—were expected.

We also probably knew that life might seem unfair sometimes. So what? If it's fair, it's not a true trial.[23] We chose to come to earth with full agency, knowing we would sin and experience its painful consequences, because we knew this was the only way for us to grow.

While choices often have permanent and sometimes painful consequences, every trial can ultimately be for our own good. Paul wrote, "All things work together for good to them that love God, to them who are called according to his purpose" (Romans 8:28). And "all things" includes our trials and afflictions—even the consequences of weak or flawed decisions. Lehi echoed this promise to his son Jacob when he said that God would "consecrate [his] afflictions for [his] gain" (2 Nephi 2:2).

My brother Coulter learned firsthand how, when you love God, even the most severe trials can lead to miraculous blessings. As a missionary in El Salvador, Coulter lived in some of the poorest, most dangerous cities in the world. Coulter is the youngest of eight boys who have all served missions, but none of us (not even my brother Clint, who served a mission in the freezing Sapporo, Japan) experienced anything near Coulter's level of physical adversity.

Coulter was robbed at gunpoint dozens of times, had gangs interrupt discussions to threaten families he was teaching, saw multiple people killed by gunfire, was fired at in a drive-by shooting (in which his companion got shot in the leg), got sick countless times from rotten food, was hospitalized for dengue fever, and broke out with shingles that hurt so bad he couldn't sleep.

Here's the letter Coulter wrote when he got shingles. He had been out a little over a year, and this was his lowest point:

January 21, 2013

Nothing worse than a week where almost every single lesson fell through, and I got shingles. But it's all good! More trials, more opportunities to grow. This week was also rough as always . . . I really am giving it my all. It's all over my back so I can't sleep, which is really garbage. Shingles is the pits. . . . Really I don't know what to write, this week was killer. I really don't want to be Debbie Downer and don't want you guys to think that the mission isn't amazing, just sometimes it's difficult, and this week was the most difficult of my life. Okay, I just read all that and probably should erase it all. The mission is the best thing I've ever done. I love it and wouldn't trade this week for anything in the world. I love you guys. . . . You all are in my prayers and thoughts each and every day. The Church is so true. If I wasn't sure of this I wouldn't be here. But I can say without a doubt it is true. We are so blessed. In my worst moments this week I was so blessed to know I always have someone I can turn to and just need to drop to my knees.

Love, Elder Reynolds

Exactly three months later, Coulter sent the following letter:

April 21, 2013

I have never had a happier day in my whole mission. Without a doubt. Yesterday was marvelous. My heart is still in shreds. I was blessed with thirty-five baptisms yesterday. Usually one or two for companionship every month is normal . . . but the zone worked together and put the high goal of 100 baptisms in one [month], which would make us the highest baptizing zone in the world. I worked harder the last seven weeks than I think I have my whole life put together. I've never been more stressed either . . . but man . . . the blessings were so worth it. I love the mission. It was absolutely amazing. I baptized more people in one day than I have in my whole mission. But it doesn't end there. After my baptismal service I got permission from the president to go to my first area, which I loved so much . . . to baptize my first investigator. I cannot express the joy I had when I entered the waters of baptism with someone that I challenged to be baptized in my first week in the mission. My FIRST investigator. When I saw her and her family I just fell apart. It was such a grand blessing from the Lord. I cannot express. No words can express the joy I felt this day. I also got to see the whole ward of La Union. The missionaries told them I was coming and they all lined up in the entrance to greet me. It was unbelievably marvelous. All my converts were there. I was so, so happy. I loved every second of it. Life is amazing. Better said, the gospel and the Lord are amazing.

Love, Elder Reynolds

These letters[24] testify that when we are humble and look to the Lord, He will consecrate afflictions for our gain. He wants to grant us miracles. We just have to let Him.

Resisting Temptation Strengthens Spiritual Muscles

Following the path of least resistance is a natural law of physics. Rivers travel through the lowest valleys, and electricity in thunderclouds seeks the tallest tree. A corollary to this law is that resistance produces strength. Athletes who train at high altitude have an advantage over those who don't, and those who lift heavier weights build stronger muscles. President Kimball wrote: "The supreme reward of struggle is strength. Life is a battle and the greatest joy is to overcome. The pursuit of easy things makes men weak. . . . It is following the lines of least resistance that makes rivers and men crooked."[25]

Sin works the same way. The more you build resistance against temptation, the less impact it can have over you. Just as physical resistance builds physical strength, spiritual resistance to temptation builds spiritual strength. Accordingly, as Elder Maxwell wrote, "If you're not tested, make up your mind to not amount to much."[26]

> Just as physical resistance builds physical strength, spiritual resistance to temptation builds spiritual strength.

I've witnessed this principle in action with Brandon Flowers. While working with the Killers over the last eleven years, I've seen that twenty- to thirty-year-old assaulted by an impossible amount of temptation. Yet—while Brandon insists he isn't perfect—he is often taking difficult steps to avoid his more enticing sins. For example, instead of going to the band's after parties when a concert ends, he is usually on the tour bus or in his hotel room working on new songs. In short, when he can avoid hanging out in a bar, he does.

In the summer of 2013, when we were in Moscow, Brandon

spoke to a congregation of Mormon youth. After one boy's question was translated—"How do you avoid so much temptation when you are in a rock band on the road?"—Brandon gave an answer I will never forget: "It gets easier." Later that year in Taiwan, he was asked a similar question and repeated the same simple testimony. *When you are committed to avoiding temptation, "it gets easier."*

President Benson described this phenomenon, saying, "When obedience ceases to be an irritant and becomes our quest, in that moment God will endow us with power."[27] A humble rock star's commitment to obey God gave him more power to resist temptation than any human could have on his or her own.

I understand that, particularly at first, resisting temptation isn't fun or easy. It reminds me of going to the gym. I want to have bigger muscles, and I know that lifting heavy weights is the way to get them. But it's hard to get into that routine. It's hard to commit yourself to struggling against anything. Yet, as Brandon put it, I do know that it gets easier.

> When you are committed to avoiding temptation, "it gets easier."

Remember, we wanted trials so that we could grow. We "shouted for joy" at the opportunity to pass through the veil and experience temptations, pain, and adversity (Job 38:7). We fought for this right. Yet sometimes we forget where we are or why we are here. *We pick up a weight and act disappointed to find it isn't light.*

God Can Transform Weaknesses into Strengths

As a further miracle of the Atonement, trials don't result in just a generalized spiritual strength. With God's grace, specific weaknesses can become their diametrically opposed strengths (see

Ether 12:27). It is amazing that the Lord doesn't simply reduce our weaknesses. Instead, He literally turns them into strengths.

This miracle is on par with raising Lazarus from the dead or giving sight to the blind, and God wants to grant it to *you.*

Perhaps the Greatest Spiritual Strengths Were All Once Weaknesses

In a recent general conference, Elder David A. Bednar announced, "Without that strengthening power of the Atonement, I could not stand before you this morning."[28] Ammon similarly recognized he was "nothing" and as to his own strength "weak," yet he boasted in God, exclaiming, "In his strength I can do all things" (Alma 26:12).

Perhaps all of the most powerful spiritual strengths we have record of were once, before the Lord's intervention, corresponding weaknesses.

The Words of Isaiah, Moses, and Enoch

In the Old Testament, Christianity's foundation is formed by the words of two prophets: Isaiah and Moses. The Savior declared "great are the words of Isaiah" (3 Nephi 23:1), and He quoted Isaiah more than any other prophet. From the mouth of Moses came the law of Moses, including the Ten Commandments. Ironically, both of these men had been ashamed of their weaknesses in speech. Moses repeatedly described himself as "of uncircumcised lips" and "slow of speech, and of a slow tongue" (Exodus 6:30; Exodus 4:10). Before an angel purified him with a hot coal from the altar, Isaiah considered himself "a man of unclean lips" (Isaiah 6:5).

Speech was also a humbling weakness for Enoch. "All the people hate me," he wrote, "for I am slow of speech" (Moses 6:31). Measured by the effect of his words, however, Enoch's prophetic ability to inspire could be considered unparalleled. He and his followers were raised to heaven, to be reunited with those on Earth under the millennial reign of Jesus Christ (see Moses 7:69). Some of those followers include the people of Melchizedek, who had previously "all gone astray" and "were full of all manner of wickedness" (Alma 13:17; Joseph Smith Translation, Genesis 14:34).

Moroni's Writing

Similar to Isaiah, Moses, and Enoch facing difficulties in speaking, the prophet Moroni was humbled by his weakness in writing. After reading the articulate writings of the brother of Jared, Moroni felt inadequate "because of the awkwardness of [his] hands" (Ether 12:24). Worried that his weakness would harm the Lord's work, he exclaimed, "When we write we behold our weakness, and stumble because of the placing of our words; and I fear lest the Gentiles shall mock at our words" (Ether 12:25).

Despite his former weakness, however, the Lord chose Moroni to edit numerous chapters and the title page of the "most correct of any book on earth."[29] Moreover, the introduction to the Book of Mormon contains only one scripture: Moroni 10:3–5. Moroni's written words remain the most quoted scripture by missionaries and the promise whereby we determine the truth of the Book of Mormon and the restored gospel. Surely the Lord transformed any weakness Moroni had in writing into an unparalleled strength.

Joseph Smith's Writing

Joseph in Egypt prophesied of "a choice seer . . . and unto him will I give power to bring forth my word . . . and out of weakness he shall be made strong" (2 Nephi 3:7,11,13). "I raised you up," the Lord told that seer (Joseph Smith Jr.), "that I might show forth my wisdom through the weak things of the earth" (D&C 124:1).

In fact, Joseph Smith did not start off as a gifted writer, and he was well aware of his weakness. In his own words (revealing much), Joseph said he was "deprived of the bennifit of an education suffice it to say [he] was mearly instructtid in reading writing and the ground rules of Arithmatic."[30] Emma, Joseph's wife, said Joseph "could neither write nor dictate a coherent and well-worded letter; let alone dictat[e] a book like the Book of Mormon."[31]

But once the Lord turned Joseph's weakness into a strength, the prophet was able to translate and write down "more holy scripture than any single prophet who ever lived" and, as Elder Bruce R. McConkie proclaimed, "has preserved for us more of the mind and will and voice of the Lord than the total of the dozen most prolific prophetic penmen of the past."[32]

The Missionary Efforts of Paul, Alma the Younger, and the Sons of Mosiah

With fourteen epistles and multiple long missions, the Apostle Paul was arguably the most influential missionary of the New Testament. Prior to his change of heart, though, Paul "persecuted the church of God" "beyond measure" (Galatians 1:13), even standing by and guarding the clothes of the witnesses while Stephen was stoned, and "consenting unto his death" (Acts 22:20).

The greatest missionaries of the Book of Mormon also once possessed the opposing spiritual weakness. Before his conversion, Alma the Younger was "a very wicked and an idolatrous man," so deeply ensnared by the devil that he and the sons of Mosiah spoke "much flattery to the people" and did all they could to "destroy the church" (Mosiah 27:8, 10).

After his change of heart, however, Alma became the leader of the Church and the chief judge and leader of the entire Nephite people (see Mosiah 29:42). The sons of Mosiah went on to serve perhaps the most difficult yet effective missions in recorded history.

The Faith of the Brother of Jared

The brother of Jared was chosen to lead the Jaredites to America (see Ether 2:7). However, when the Jaredites reached the shore, instead of crossing the sea, they pitched their tents and stayed—and not just for a few months. They stayed for four years, all because the brother of Jared "remembered not" to faithfully "call upon the name of the lord" (Ether 2:13–14).

After being chastized by the Lord, however (see Ether 2:14), the brother of Jared became one of the "greatest of God's prophets forever."[33] The Lord himself proclaimed, "Never has man believed in me as thou hast" (Ether 3:15).

The same prophet who once took four years to ask directions became so bold as to ask the Lord to show Himself, resulting in one of the "greatest moments in recorded faith."[34]

> We all can have our weaknesses turned into their opposing strengths.

Whether we have common imperfections and struggles with faith or are plagued by the most grave of weaknesses, *we all can have our weaknesses turned into their opposing strengths.*

President Benson exclaimed, "What a promise from the Lord! The very source of our troubles can be changed, molded, and formed into a strength and a source of power."[35]

As set forth in the following chapters, a change of heart—whether mighty and instantaneous or gradual and gentle—is the process whereby our weaknesses become strengths.

KEY POINTS

GOD CAN TURN YOUR WEAKNESSES INTO STRENGTHS

1. Trials, afflictions, and even mistakes can be consecrated for our gain and bring miraculous blessings.

2. Trials strengthen spiritual muscles, empowering us to better fight and endure future trials and temptation.

3. God can turn our weaknesses into monumental strengths.

4. Many of the greatest spiritual strengths were, at one time, weaknesses.

5. Weaknesses are changed into strengths by the process of a mighty change of heart, or sanctification.

PART TWO

HOW TO OBTAIN A MIGHTY CHANGE OF HEART

CHAPTER 3

THE MIGHTY CHANGE

A heart transplant can prolong life for years for
people who would otherwise die from heart failure. But it
is not "the ultimate operation," as Time *magazine called*
it in 1967. The ultimate operation is not a physical
but a spiritual "mighty change" of heart.

ELDER DALE G. RENLUND[36]

A s we learned in chapter 1, repetitive sin hardens our hearts. We don't want to feel guilty for choices we know are wrong. And the Holy Spirit's pangs are uncomfortable. Thus, seeking to avoid discomfort, our hearts grow hard. This is a spiritually perilous situation.

With a hardened heart, we can become past feeling. The soft whispers of the Spirit cannot reach us in the ways we need (and, though we may not yet realize it, the ways we truly want). This happens to the best of us.

So what can we do? By ourselves, not much. The Lord, however, can replace a stony heart with a new heart. Ezekiel reads, "A new heart also will I give you, and a new spirit will I put within you: and I will take away the stony heart out of your flesh, and I will give you an heart of flesh" (Ezekiel 36:26).

New hearts are once again susceptible to the Holy Spirit's counsel and influence, and they develop an aversion to temptation. This is called a "mighty change of heart." After you experience a mighty change of heart, the sins that once plagued you can become far less tempting (perhaps not tempting at all!), and weaknesses can become strengths.

Mighty changes of heart are for egregious and minor sinners alike. But in reality, that is a useless distinction. As James explained, even if you obey every commandment except one (as if that were possible), it's the same as if you were "guilty of all" (James 2:10). Regardless of the size or number of sins, like holes in our individual lifeboats, "the terrible truth is that each of us is sinking . . . each of us needs the Savior as much as anyone else does."[37]

Because we are all repetitive sinners in sinking lifeboats, as Elder David A. Bednar proclaimed, a mighty change of heart is something we all must receive: "Repenting of our sins and seeking forgiveness are spiritually necessary, and we must always do so. But remission of sin is not the only or even the ultimate purpose of the gospel. To have our hearts changed by the Holy Spirit such that 'we have no more disposition to do evil, but to do good continually' (Mosiah 5:2), as did King Benjamin's people, is the covenant responsibility we have accepted."[38]

To have our hearts changed so that we lose our desire to sin is a covenant responsibility.

Step back and think about this. That temptation provoking your habitual, repetitive sin can become abhorrent! The mighty change is not only about becoming more able to battle personal temptation; it is about making those temptations undesirable. In other words, after a mighty change of heart, you could see formerly enticing temptations as a vegetarian sees roast beef.

Does that not sound fantastic?

In *A Christmas Carol,* the "covetous old sinner"[39] Ebenezer Scrooge experienced what seems to be a mighty change of heart.[40] After a supernatural experience (visits from Jacob Marley and the

Ghosts of Christmas Past, Present, and Yet to Come), Ebenezer transforms from a greedy miser, who overworked and underpaid his clerk Bob Cratchit, into a hallmark of charity—"as good a man, as the good old city knew, or any other good old city, town, or borough, in the good old world."[41]

What did Ebenezer do to deserve this mighty change? Is there a missing chapter in *A Christmas Carol*? He had been nothing but a selfish, greedy sinner.

Then again, what do any of us do to deserve our Savior's grace? No one "deserves" the fruits of the Atonement, or any other miracle. Even if we were to serve God "with all [our] whole souls yet [we] would be unprofitable servants" (Mosiah 2:21).

Alma the Younger recognized that he did not merit his own mighty change, stating, "If I had not been born of God I should not have known these things; but God has, by the mouth of his holy angel, made these things known unto me, *not of any worthiness of myself*" (Alma 36:5; emphasis added).

> To have our hearts changed so that we lose our desire to sin is a covenant responsibility.

None of us deserves a spiritual heart transplant. If anyone could deserve that change, perhaps it would be those who are affected by the consequences of others' choices, such as Bob Cratchit's son Tiny Tim or the Church members persecuted by Alma the Younger, Saul/Paul, or the sons of Mosiah.

Although we don't deserve God's miraculous intervention in our lives, Moroni revealed two prerequisites to receiving it: "If men come unto me I will show unto them their weakness. I give unto men weakness that they may be humble; and my grace is sufficient for all men that humble themselves before me; for if they *humble themselves before me,* and *have faith in me,* then will I make weak things become strong unto them" (Ether 12:27; emphasis added).

So, to experience a mighty change of heart and have our weaknesses transformed into strengths, we must (1) humble ourselves and (2) have faith in Christ.

Gradual changes of heart, part of the process known as "sanctification" (see Moses 6:59–60), are built upon identical principles. Like the more rapid "mighty change of heart," the process of sanctification similarly changes our desires to not "look upon sin save it were with abhorrence" (Alma 13:12). Describing this process, Mormon wrote: "They did fast and pray oft, and did wax *stronger and stronger in their humility,* and *firmer and firmer in the faith of Christ,* unto the filling their souls with joy and consolation, yea, even to the purifying and the *sanctification of their hearts,* which sanctification cometh because of their yielding their hearts unto God" (Helaman 3:35; emphasis added).

Multiple scriptures have made this clear. There are two prerequisites for both mighty and gradual changes of heart: strong humility and firm faith.

If someone said that faith and humility were virtually identical, at first you'd disagree, right? I was shocked to discover how related these concepts actually are. Humility involves realizing how much we rely upon the Savior. Faith involves humbly relying upon the Savior. Thus there is inevitable overlap. Considering the repeated emphasis on humility throughout the scriptures and words of the prophets, we probably need it. Why do all of the greatest strengths seem to originate as weaknesses? Maybe because the greatest strengths are gifts—and while "God resisteth the proud," His greatest gifts are reserved for "the humble" (James 4:6).

Notwithstanding the overlap between faith and humility, we'll use this distinction: humility involves *recognizing* our weaknesses and the accompanying need to rely solely upon the Lord, and faith involves *acting* upon that recognition. Humility is about knowing you ought to rely; faith is actually relying.

KEY POINTS

A MIGHTY CHANGE OF HEART

1. God can replace our hard hearts (hearts past feeling) with new hearts.

2. New hearts are once again susceptible to the Holy Spirit's counsel and influence, and they develop an aversion to temptation. In other words, repetitive sins that once plagued us may no longer even tempt us.

3. A mighty change of heart (or sanctification) is a divine gift we may receive upon meeting the conditions of strong humility and firm faith.

CHAPTER 4

THE FIRST PREREQUISITE: STRONG HUMILITY

*Do you find yourself hating what you are doing but
not able to find the willpower to turn away from it?
Then reach out and humble yourself. The Lord's enabling
power is sufficient to change your heart, to turn your life,
to purge your soul. But you must make the first move,
which is to humble yourself and realize that
only in God can you find deliverance.*

M. RUSSELL BALLARD[42]

The second chapter in the Book of Mormon describes an "exceedingly young" Nephi who believed his father's teachings and "[cried] unto the Lord" (1 Nephi 2:16). As a consequence of this humility, the Lord visited him and "did soften [his heart]" (1 Nephi 2:16). In contrast, Nephi's older brothers "rebel[led] against" the teachings of their father (the prophet at the time) and experienced "hardness of their hearts" (1 Nephi 2:18). From that second chapter forward, the Book of Mormon repeatedly illustrates the consequences of hardening and softening hearts.

Each time, we see that "the first move" in obtaining a soft or new heart, as Elder Ballard put it, is strong humility (see Helaman 3:35). Even for those who already consider themselves humble—perhaps a warning sign?—this step is harder than it sounds. For me, at least, pride sneaks its way in through cracks I hadn't noticed and ways I never would have expected.

Strong Humility Entails Recognizing Our Weakness and Our Dependence on the Lord's Grace

The story of the Zoramites on Rameumptom is chosen for our day. Like many religious adherents (ourselves included), they too thought they were "a chosen and holy people" (Alma 31:18). The Zoramites were pleased with their level of righteousness and religious stature. This attitude is the opposite of what we need to receive a mighty change of heart. It is the opposite of strong humility.

Instead of focusing on our own comparative (and pitiful, if we're being honest) levels of righteousness, we are required to recognize "a sense of [our] nothingness, and [our] worthless and fallen state" (Mosiah 4:5). Like Ammon, we need to confess that we are "nothing" because "as to [our] strength [we are] weak" (Alma 26:12). Like Moses, we must "know that man is nothing, which thing [he] never had supposed" (Moses 1:10). Like Nephi and King Benjamin, we have to recognize that so "great is the nothingness of the children of men" that we "are less than the dust of the earth" (Helaman 12:7; Mosiah 4:2).

The word of God could not be clearer. Perhaps willpower alone will suffice when it comes to obeying many of the commandments. But when we are faced with the sins we "enjoy"— those repeated sins that mirror our individual weaknesses— personal discipline is not enough. If you could have overcome your habitual, repetitive sins by yourself, you would have done so already. You didn't, and you couldn't, because we *can't*. Alone, we are just too weak.

And that's okay. It's okay to be in this "worthless and fallen" state. You are not supposed to just set better goals, read a better self-help book, and shout "I can do it!" You are supposed to realize that, alone, you can't do it. Particularly when it comes to our greatest challenges—we will repeatedly fail until we recognize that no matter how hard we try to obey, our "righteousnesses are as filthy rags" (Isaiah 64:6) compared to what we can accomplish through our Father's enabling grace (see Mosiah 4:5–7).

After all, even Christ did not just make it on His own. At times, He withdrew from the multitudes to pray to His Father. Despite unparalleled righteousness, He still "continued from grace to grace" (D&C 93:13). And in Gethsemane, as He prayed, an angel came to strengthen Him (see Luke 22:43). *Even our sinless Savior needed strength beyond His own and power from our Heavenly Father.*

This recognition is the heart of strong humility.

Is Strong Humility Easy?

I never said it would be easy,
I only said it would be worth it.

In my neighbor's freshman dorm room at BYU hung a poster of Jesus with the above quote written across it. The poster is common and still available for sale in various LDS and other Christian bookstores. But despite the claim of many, Christ never said those words. The thought is catchy, but is it true?

We know the necessary level of humility for the Atonement's change of heart is worth it. Whether it is easy, however, is more complicated. On one hand, strong humility is hard to obtain. It isn't comfortable to see yourself in a "worthless and fallen state" (Mosiah 4:5). Neither is it easy to relinquish any degree of spiritual independence. Our identities are formed, in part, by making different decisions from those around us. Transitioning into adulthood, teenage rebellion is the natural consequence of adolescents no longer wanting to be treated like children. Talk about fodder for rock music—from "Girls Just Want to Have Fun" by

Cyndi Lauper to "(You Gotta) Fight For Your Right to Party" by the Beastie Boys, there must be a thousand songs in every generation about standing up to authority and how "Parents Just Don't Understand."[43] It is instinctive for us to embrace our individuality and resist following rules.

This instinct has been around since the mud of creation. Remember, our moral agency was a hard-fought premortal victory. We are understandably reluctant to lower our voices in that battle cry, let alone surrender.

With the right frame of mind, however, obtaining strong humility can be easy.

After all, Christ said His "yoke is easy and [His] burden is light" (Matthew 11:30). We know a yoke is a wooden frame or bar with loops at either end, fitted around the necks of a pair of animals. Figuratively, a yoke involves servitude (something that does not sound easy). It also represents a coupling, a state of working together (like a marriage relationship), in which we are yoked to the Lord.

To take Christ's yoke is to enter into a voluntary state of subjection and surrender to His will. Remember, King Benjamin said that we must do more than be "submissive"; we must be "willing to submit." *We need to want it.* And—here is the key—*when we* want *to go where He goes, being yoked with the Savior is easy.*

Christ's Yoke Is Easy Because It Is for Our Own Good

Christ's yoke is easy when we humbly *choose* His will because then we are only doing what we want. We aren't keeping commandments begrudgingly or out of fear, but out of love and desire. Thinking about it rationally, we are choosing to follow the most perfect guide to our own happiness (see John 14:15; see also Matthew 22:37; Mark 12:30). Rebellion and reluctant acquiescence are not factors when the decision to submit to God's will is what we truly want.

Christ's yoke is also easy because He never prohibits anything unless it's for our own benefit. We will not avoid every trial, but *with Christ's yoke, the trials we experience will ultimately lead to good.* As the Lord told the Prophet Joseph, referring to even the most intense adversity, "All these things shall give thee experience, and shall be for thy good" (D&C 122:7). George Q. Cannon also explained, "I know that everything will be overruled for our good if we do right. No matter how difficult circumstances may be to bear at the time, they are for our good and God watches over us; His angels are round about us all the time."[44]

This is why our hard hearts need to break. We must realize that doing things our way, with rules tweaked as we see fit— whether that be choosing to date before the age of sixteen, having "just a couple of beers every now and then," or being dishonest in a business deal— never produces desirable outcomes. In the end, every path of our own creation will lead to less happiness and more captivity.

> When we *want* to go where He goes, being yoked with the Savior is easy.

This was the most important lesson I learned as a missionary. Trying to serve a mission while holding on to any "off-the-plan" behavior is a nightmare. You can flirt and watch TV, or you can serve a mission. You can't do both. As the Savior Himself taught, "No man can serve two masters" (Matthew 6:24).

Maybe you can get away with something here or there, but missionaries who disobey grow increasingly unhappy and frustrated and always ultimately suffer negative consequences—either during their missions or later in life when they realize their missed opportunities.

In contrast, missionaries who are "willing to submit" to all of the mission rules have far better experiences. They are universally happier. And their mission experiences benefit them for the rest of their lives.

Our lives outside a full-time mission are the same. Forging our own path in opposition to God's will is not just prideful, it is ignorant. As Elder L. Tom Perry explained, choosing to follow Him "is a choice between our own limited knowledge and power and God's unlimited wisdom and omnipotence."[45] The right choice should be obvious. Relying upon only our own judgment, we have no idea which paths will bring the most happiness, health, or success. Every important choice is affected by things outside our control or foreknowledge. Natural disasters, early deaths, the state of the economy, and the success or failure of business pursuits will drastically impact our lives—for better or for worse.

From psychics and palm readers, who have been around for thousands of years, to the Magic 8-Balls found on the shelves today, mankind has always been obsessed with predicting the future. We would love to know where different paths would lead us in order to make informed decisions, but we have no clue. Yet *He knows.* We could receive an unexpected inheritance or win the lottery. Alternatively, we could get hit by a bus tomorrow. With the Lord's infinite love and foreknowledge, it doesn't take much to recognize we want Him on our team. We want Him in our yoke because with His perfect knowledge, He can help us get where we ultimately want to go.

Christ's Yoke Is Easy Because He Shares Our Burdens, Making Them Light

A second reason why the Savior's yoke is easy is that when we are yoked by His side, He shares our burdens. In the Book of Mormon, when Amulon forced the people of Alma into captivity and imposed severe restrictions on them, the Lord could have rescued them. Instead, He promised to "ease the burdens which are put upon your shoulders, that even you cannot feel them upon your backs, even while you are in bondage" (Mosiah 24:14). Because their "burdens . . . were made light . . . they could bear up their burdens with ease," and the people of Alma were able to "submit cheerfully" (Mosiah 24:15).

> With Christ's yoke, the trials we experience will ultimately lead to good.

This story stands in contrast to what happened with Limhi's people. Ironically, only a few years earlier, both groups were subjects of King Noah. And after King Noah suffered death by fire, both groups were made slaves. Exactly like they did with the people of Alma, the Lamanites began to "exercise authority over [the people of Limhi]; . . . and began to put heavy burdens upon their backs, and drive them as they would a dumb ass" (Mosiah 21:3).

Unlike Alma's followers, who were yoked to Christ and relied upon His strength, Limhi's people tried to remove the burdens themselves. On three different occasions they battled the Lamanites, and each time "they were driven back again, suffering much loss" (Mosiah 21:11). Only when they were "desirous to become even as Alma and his brethren" and "willing to serve God with all their hearts" were their burdens made light and ultimately removed (Mosiah 21:34–35).

Whether the Lord actually lessens our burdens or makes them feel lighter by strengthening our ability to bear them, He helps us bear our burdens with greater ease. Lehi's family experienced this when they endured "much affliction in the wilderness" for eight years, yet their affliction was not unbearable (1 Nephi 17:1). Joseph Smith also received comfort during his most burdensome time in Liberty Jail. "My son, peace be unto thy soul," said the Lord, "thine adversity and thine afflictions shall be but a small moment " (D&C 121:7).

We cannot bear the burdens of this world alone. When we are yoked with Christ, however, through His strength and with "strong . . . humility," we can gain from our trials, have our burdens made light, and turn our weaknesses into strengths (Ether 12:27). We should want our hard hearts to break and to humbly submit to the Lord's will in all things because only then will "all things"—not some things, but *all things*—work together for [our] good" (Romans 8:28).

God Loves Us So Much That Sometimes He Helps (or Compels) Us to Feel Humble

Our Heavenly Father does more than change our hearts when we meet the conditions of humility and faith. He also loves us so much that He helps us meet those conditions. *He encourages strong humility by giving us weakness and through acts of divine intervention.*

Remember that promise made by God: "If men come unto me I will show unto them their weakness. I give unto men weakness that they may be humble" (Ether 12:27).

There are two unusual concepts here. First, God doesn't just "show" us our weakness, He gives it to us. To clarify, the Lord gives us weakness in the sense that we live in mortal bodies in a fallen world; the Lord does not cause anyone to sin. Rather, we choose sin when we succumb to our personal weaknesses instead of surrendering to the Savior. As James taught, "Let no man say when he is tempted, I am tempted of God: for God cannot be tempted with evil, neither tempteth he any man: But every man is tempted, when he is drawn away of his own lust, and enticed" (James 1:13–14).

Second, it is unusual to think of weaknesses as blessings. Elder M. Russell Ballard explains: "If we were perfect in every respect, it would be hard to be humble. Even in specific things, humility comes harder to those who are very strong in one area or another. The woman or man who is remarkably beautiful or handsome can easily become proud of her or his appearance. A brilliant scholar may look down in condescension on those less intellectually blessed. Our weaknesses help us to be humble."[46]

Ideally, our weaknesses will humble us sufficiently before our lives unravel. But, one way or the other, sin's bondage will ultimately get our attention. Sometimes these consequences involve ecclesiastical or legal ramifications. Sometimes sin's consequences are more personally painful and severe. Regardless, while it is better for us to "humble [our]selves" than to be "compelled to be humble" (Alma 32:14), being compelled to be humble is a blessing nonetheless.

Hitting Rock Bottom

Nephi explained that the Atonement's grace (including the mighty change of heart) applies "unto all those who have a broken heart and a contrite spirit; and unto none else" (2 Nephi 2:7). There is no way of getting around this. Remember, we are all repetitive sinners; we will experience hardened hearts, and we will need our hearts changed. This cannot occur without brokenhearted humility. *Apparently, like any item with a warranty from its manufacturer, hard hearts must break before they can be replaced.*

In addiction therapy, that depth of humility is sometimes referred to as "hitting rock bottom."[47] We don't have to wait until our lives fall apart before we become sufficiently humble, by the way. That's like waiting for a heart attack before getting that needed bypass surgery. Unfortunately, many of us are too stubborn to recognize bondage until the most serious consequences occur.

I recently helped a twenty-five-year-old guy who had hit rock bottom overcome an opiate addiction. Let's call him Joey. One day I saw Joey melt heroin and speed on a tin can and shoot up in a Best Buy parking lot. Two weeks later, he was clean. Although I doubted he could do this without a rehab facility, I saw it happen.

This all started with an offer to buy a homeless kid lunch. Pale, nauseous, and curled up, this guy was "dopesick"—so deep into his addiction that he couldn't even eat until he injected brown liquid into a barely viable vein. "Are you high?" I asked after he put the paraphernalia back in his pack.

"Are you kidding me? I can't even remember the last time I got high," he said. "I'm a maintenance user, man. I need drugs just to maintain." Unlike other repeated sins, getting off of heroin can literally kill you.

Because I'm interested in how to solve the problem of homelessness, I asked Joey for advice. I asked him to imagine that he had $10,000,000 to start a charity to help the homeless and addicts. I wanted to know what he would do to make a difference. To my surprise, he said he would do nothing. He said that plenty of resources were already available. He described two past girlfriends who had unsuccessfully tried to get off drugs. "When people really want to change, they will," he said. "They just didn't want it bad enough back then. People into this stuff don't need bailing out," he said. "They need to hit bottom."

After years of addiction, Joey felt compelled to change, and he credited this permanent change with one thing: hitting rock bottom. He finally decided he wasn't going to spend another day unable to eat without first needing to use $100 worth of drugs. The cost of his weakness finally became intolerable.

Acts of Divine Intervention

Sometimes, the Lord goes so far as to influence humility by angelic intervention. For example, Alma the Younger, Laman and Lemuel, and others were repeatedly rebuked by angels and the voice of God. This was necessary because "there was nothing save it were the power of God, which threatened them with destruction, could soften their hearts" (1 Nephi 18:20).

> Heavenly Father encourages strong humility by giving us weakness and through acts of divine intervention.

More than once, the Lord has also used famine to provoke humility. Alma the Younger's great-grandson Nephi prayed for a famine to humble his people unto repentance (see Helaman 11:4). And it worked! After the people "saw that they were about to perish by famine . . . they began to remember the Lord their God" (v. 7).

This same incentive occurred with the Nephites, who were "smitten with famine and sore afflictions, to stir them up in remembrance of their duty" (Mosiah 1:17), and the Jaredites, who received a famine and "poisonous serpents" (Ether 9:31). Then, as so commonly occurs, "when the people saw that they must perish they began to repent of their iniquities and cry unto the Lord" (v. 34).

It is no wonder that the word "disaster" has Latin roots—*dis* + *astrum*—that mean "from the stars."[48] Ancient civilizations that attributed famines, floods, and other disasters to the heavens were, at least some of the time, right. In the last days, the Lord mentions other types of famines that may not be "a famine of bread, nor a thirst for water" (Amos 8:11). Losing a job or affection from a loved one can be a motivational famine if it helps us humbly recognize our dependence on the Lord.

War has also been used by the Lord to humble His children. The book of Alma records that "many had become hardened, because of the exceedingly great length of the war," yet at the same time "many were softened because of their afflictions, insomuch that they did humble themselves before God, even in the depth of humility" (Alma 62:41).

In Alma the Younger's mission to the Zoramites, he found people humbled by poverty (see Alma 32: 4–5). Instead of feeling sorry for them, Alma was full of joy because he "beheld that their afflictions had truly humbled them" (v. 6). He told them: "It is well that ye are cast out of your synagogues, that ye may be humble . . . for it is because that ye are cast out, that ye are despised of your brethren because of your exceeding poverty, that ye are brought to a lowliness of heart; for ye are necessarily brought to be humble. And now, *because ye are compelled to be humble blessed are ye;* for a man sometimes, if he is compelled to be humble, seeketh repentance" (vv. 12–13; emphasis added).[49]

> Like any item with a warranty from its manufacturer, hard hearts must break before they can be replaced.

Of course, no famine, war, angelic visitation, poverty, or other affliction will necessarily produce broken-hearted humility. Even with divine intervention, our agency is never compromised. As Alma explains, only "sometimes, if he is compelled to be humble" does a man seek repentance (Alma 32:13). Remember, even the most extreme examples of angelic visitations to Laman and Lemuel, including being physically shaken by the power of God, did not cause them to become humble (see 1 Nephi 3:29–30; 17:45–54). Our natural inclination toward hard-heartedness is shocking indeed.

> If we want to make permanent, real changes in our lives, we must seize those opportunities for humility when they arise.

Nephi, son of Helaman, must have felt this frustration when, after praying for a famine that led to repentance, he bemoaned our pitiful forgetfulness: "And thus we see that except the Lord doth chasten his people with many afflictions, yea, except he doth visit them with death and with terror, and with famine and with all manner of pestilence, they will not remember him" (Helaman 12:3).

In short, the Lord loves us so much that He will, at times, visit us with death, terror, famine, and "all manner of pestilence." *If we want to make permanent, real changes in our lives, we must seize those opportunities for humility when they arise.*

Whether we hit rock bottom due to the dramatic consequences of sinful behavior or a divinely directed "famine" or we recognize our weaknesses by their inescapable cycle of behavior—of commission or omission—we should thank the Lord for giving us appropriate perspective and humility. This is the first prerequisite, or essential step, toward a mighty change of heart.

KEY POINTS

STRONG HUMILITY

1. We need to humbly realize that our ability to overcome repetitive sins without the Lord's grace is too weak.

2. Submitting to our Savior's will is easier when we realize that the commandments are for our own good, that they lead to what we will ultimately want, and that the Savior makes our burdens light.

3. Sometimes the Lord helps encourage humility by letting us experience the consequences of sin and/or through acts of divine intervention.

CHAPTER 5

THE SECOND PREREQUISITE: FIRM FAITH

*Our lives are the only meaningful expression of
what we believe and in Whom we believe. And the only
real wealth, for any of us, lies in our faith.*

PRESIDENT GORDON B. HINCKLEY[50]

It is not surprising that a miraculous change of heart requires faith, because "it is by faith that miracles are wrought" (Moroni 7:37). Whether this miracle occurs gradually (sanctification) or instantaneously (a mighty change of heart), when we have "firm faith," the enabling power of the Lord's grace takes hold (see Helaman 3:35; see also Ether 12:27). This power of the Atonement *"helps us to overcome sin* and [is] a sanctifying and *strengthening power* that helps us to become better than we ever could by relying only upon our own strength."[51]

Put simply, "faith is a principle of action and power."[52] While humility is the willingness to rely on the Savior's grace in order to effectively obey, repent, and have our hearts changed, faith in Christ is that step of actually relying.

Faith Is Trusting the Savior Instead of Our Own Strength

In the New Testament, the word *faith* corresponds to the Greek noun *pistis* or the verb *pisteuo*, meaning "belief with the predominate idea of trust." It also involves "fidelity" or "the character of one who can be relied on."[53] The Latin origin of *faith* is *fides* or *fidere*, also meaning "to trust."[54] Clearly, faith is more than belief—even strong belief. As James noted, "the devils also believe, and tremble" (James 2:19). So how is our faith in Christ different than the belief of Satan and his minions? Trust.

When we receive the gift of faith, we don't only believe in the Savior. We trust Him; we rely upon His grace and Atonement. Unlike Satan, who fought for his own plan of happiness, those who receive the gift of faith "trust in the Lord with all [their] heart; and lean not unto [their] own understanding" (Proverbs 3:5). These humble followers of Christ trust Him more than anything.

They trust Him more than any means of physical protection, including "bow[s]" (Psalm 44:6) and "chariots" (Psalm 20:7), and more than their governments and political leaders (see Psalm 146:3; see also Isaiah 30:1–2). They trust Him more than any man (see 2 Nephi 28:31).[55] They trust Him above their riches or anything money can buy (see Proverbs 11:28). They trust Him more than their own strength or any arm of flesh (see Jeremiah 17:5; see also 2 Chronicles 32:8; Romans 8:1; Philippians 3:3; D&C 1:19). This is key: *followers of Christ even trust Him more than their own understanding or their own heart* (see Proverbs 3:5, 28:26).

Nephi put it best: "O Lord, I have trusted in thee and I will trust in thee forever. I will not put my trust in the arm of flesh; for I know that cursed is he that putteth his trust in the arm of flesh. Yea, cursed is he that putteth his trust in man or maketh flesh his arm" (2 Nephi 4:34).

None of this means that you shouldn't have physical protection, money, strength, natural instincts, or a strong mind. The point is that compared to our Savior, a "bow"—or a pistol by your nightstand—is not reliable protection from the true dangers in this life. Trusting the Savior means you accept that only His path will lead to real peace and joy, more than anything presented in film, television, music, or by the smartest intellectuals. You trust that He knows better than your friends, family, and even your own natural instincts or rational understanding when it comes to your well-being and happiness.

For me, trusting completely in the Lord has often been a difficult challenge. "Let go; let God" sounds easier and more relaxing than I've found it to be in practice. Maybe I'm too controlling, but allowing my own strength and judgment to take a backseat and giving faith the steering wheel makes me anxious. And my problem isn't ignorance. I know that God is ultimately in control. I know that He is all knowing, all powerful, perfectly loving, and wants what is in my best interest. I realize that He is standing right behind me, but the "trust fall" of faith that my strength, judgment, and emotions must undergo can still be difficult. We may find that even after making progress with humility and recognizing that we ought to rely on the Lord, we still struggle at times when it comes to faith, that ultimate reliance.

> Followers of Christ even trust Him more than their own understanding or their own heart.

Personal Righteousness and the "Arm of Flesh"

"Personal righteousness" is a concept that can be part of this problem. In short, we sometimes forget that "personal righteousness" is not entirely personal. For me, having exercised my metaphorical arm of flesh consistently over the years, I've become inclined to rely on it. And taking pleasure in different successes, at times I've given myself the credit. As is common, my self-worth has often been determined by objective measures—awards or compliments I've received—and an internal narrative about hard work paying off. I've had straight-A certificates on my wall and a letterman jacket in my closet. *I must be good on some level,* I've told myself, *because I experienced good outcomes that came from my own hard work.* So instead of thanking my Heavenly Father, in prideful moments I have smiled and flexed what I considered to be an able arm of flesh.

Conversely, when I've done poorly at something, I have internalized the blame. I have repeatedly held myself accountable for results and used that frustration and anxiety to motivate improvement the next time around. For whatever reason, it has come most naturally to place all the blame and all the credit on myself for both failures and successes in my life.

Religious matters have been no different. Focusing on spiritual discipline—how obedient I can be—is part of who I am. Like enjoying the outdoors, reading, and music, "striving to obey" is a personality trait I could type out on a résumé.

This focus on "personal righteousness" (a phrase we might need to reconsider) is also intertwined within LDS doctrine and practices. I remember my mission president saying, "All the Lord asks of us is that we do our best." Those words were intended to give us peace. As a missionary committed to being 100 percent obedient, however, I was bursting with anxiety. I would lie awake at night wondering whether I could have ridden my bike faster, more effectively prioritized my time, or resolved concerns with smarter answers and more powerful testimony. No matter how hard I tried, I knew that surely I could do a little better. And if I could do better, then I wasn't doing my best.

Looking back, I can see that my mission was a fantastic success. But like every so-called "success" in my life, it was not my own. I was the Lord's servant on His errand. It was His Spirit that converted every single investigator, not my persuasive ability or memorized scriptures. I didn't "find" people who needed the gospel; the Lord led me to them, or them to me. In retrospect, I cannot deny the reality that *every single meaningful event on my mission was divinely orchestrated.*

Riding my bike faster and prioritizing better were excellent goals. But that overwhelming pressure and trust I placed on my own ability and self-discipline—my "arm of flesh"—was a mistake. Relying on my admittedly weak mind and body, I felt anxiety. I felt anxiety because in my heart, I knew that even my "best" could not work miracles, and miracles are what missionaries need.

Intellectually, we know it is the Lord, not us, who works miracles. Yet it seems that Latter-day Saints find it particularly hard to completely surrender and place all our trust in God. Sometimes we talk and act as if we could somehow earn His miracles. Perhaps because "it is by faith that miracles are wrought" (Moroni 7:37), we emphasize ways to "earn" faith. We find comfort focusing on what we can quantify and control. Thus, we focus on our own discipline and strong-willed obedience.

To be clear, obedience is definitely important. Obedience is an expression of humble submission, that condition necessary for a mighty change of heart, and it is the fundamental expression of our love for God (see John 14:15; see also D&C 42:29). But we have to be careful. *Focusing on our own strength to obey is spiritually dangerous.* Even a well-intentioned focus on obedience can become reliance on the "arm of flesh," an act of pride—the opposite of strong humility—and a precursor to repetitive sin. If the devil can't reach us in our weaknesses, he will surely hit us in our strengths.

There are two opposing effects, equally damning. When we

focus on our own strength to obey, we will feel overly confident in that ability or rightfully depressed over our inability. With this false perspective, my daughter Ella had resigned herself to failure when she was only nine years old. Less than a year after being baptized, she came home from church having learned about the three degrees of glory. After describing what she had learned, she looked down and said, "I'm probably going to the middle one." Alone. Without her apparently perfect family. My sweet, earnest little girl was dead serious. And I bet the worst thing she had ever done was told a white lie or called her sister a "meanie."

Even at that innocent age, she thought returning to God meant perfect obedience, and already she knew she couldn't cut it. She knew she didn't have "A-level obedience," so—like it or not—the middle kingdom is where she was headed. This is terrible. We should never think we need to be "good enough" to get into heaven. And we should never think we stand a chance of being "good enough" on our own, either.

Instead of feeling confident about our relative obedience, we need to realize that when the going gets tough, we do not have what it takes. And that's okay! We are not supposed to wait until we have done all we can—relying on our own strength, judgment, and willpower—*before* God's grace intervenes. We are supposed to quit relying on our arms of flesh and seek Him from the beginning. This takes faith. Grace is not given to those who take self-righteous pleasure in their discipline or measurable obedience. Grace requires strong humility, and *only with faith in the Savior and His divine gift of grace can we effectively obey, repent, and change.*

Gideon and the Israelites

The book of Judges includes a fantastic story about God helping man have faith. God specifically intervened so His servants could rely entirely on Him instead of on the arm of flesh.

When Gideon's 32,000 men were already overmatched by 135,000 Midianites, the Lord said his army was too large (see Judges 7:1–3). "The people that are with thee are too many for me to give the Midianites into their hands," He said, "lest Israel vaunt themselves against me, saying, Mine own hand hath saved me" (v. 2). Thus, the Lord commanded that all those who were afraid should depart, leaving Gideon with only 10,000 men (see v. 3).

Then, after God reduced Gideon's army from 32,000 to 10,000, He reduced it yet again to only 300 (see Judges 7:4–8). With the Israelite army less than one percent of its original size, the proportion became one Israelite soldier for every 400 Midianite soldiers!

With the initial set of outmatched numbers, perhaps Gideon's army still had a chance of winning. Instead of praising God, they probably would have celebrated their own strength and strategy. With dramatically reduced troops, however, God ensured that Gideon and his men could only trust in Him and not their own arms of flesh, because the odds were too outrageous. God promised that "by the three hundred men who lapped I will save you," and He did (Judges 7:7). Gideon and His men did not save themselves, and they knew it; God saved them.

Why was God so concerned that Gideon's men recognize Him as the only meaningful source of their strength? God does not need our praise. Surely, He did not alter Gideon's odds just to feel good

> Focusing on our own strength to obey is spiritually dangerous.

when that small army attributed their victory to Him. Nor did our Heavenly Father create us solely to play harps on clouds hereafter, worshipping Him for eternity because He needs our admiration.

God wants us to recognize that we are His children in a fallen state who need His help *for our sake*. As President Henry B. Eyring put it, we "need strength beyond ourselves to keep the commandments in whatever circumstance life brings to us."[56] No matter how hard we try, our discipline will never be enough. In fact, *discipline* and *disciple* both have the same Latin root: *discipulus,* meaning "pupil or follower."[57] Someone with true discipline (a disciple) does not focus on his or her own strength or knowledge but instead on the source thereof—the Lord.

We need help to be humble, and so the Lord gives us weakness. We need help to obey, and so He gives us grace, His "enabling power" and "divine means of help or strength."[58] We need help to stop trusting in our own flawed opinions, judgment, and natural inclinations, and so He gives us faith. Thus we are able to "[rely] *alone* upon the merits of Christ, who [is] the *author and the finisher* of [our] faith" (Moroni 6:4; emphasis added).

Having Faith Is "Hard to Do" Because You Don't "Do" It— Faith Is a Gift

We know faith is a principle of action, but how you go about "doing it" is often misunderstood. In fact, faith is not simply the first thing we "do" on our heavenly chore list, because *faith is something we receive.*

As a southern-states missionary, I was constantly teaching that "faith without works is dead." James 2:14–26 repeats this idea three times. We tell ourselves that, unlike other Christians, Latter-day Saints don't merely pay lip service to the Savior's teachings (see Matthew 7:21). Instead, we try to actually keep His commandments (or at least we think so).

We are not foolish men with houses built on sand—those who hear Christ's words but don't follow them—we strive to actually do what He taught and thereby have a firm foundation (see Matthew 7:24–27). At least that's what we tell ourselves.

And yet, by what power are we able to do His will? By our own willpower? Not hardly. Even if we served God with our whole souls we would still be "unprofitable servants" (Mosiah 2:21). We owe every breath to Him, let alone the power to overcome temptation. Perhaps, when we try our hardest, we have strength enough to overcome a fair percentage of our transgressions. But when it comes to habitual, repeated sins—those sins we struggle time and time again to overcome—we are just too weak alone. We need His grace, His faith.

> Only with faith in the Savior and His divine gift of grace can we effectively obey, repent, and change.

Like everything of worth, faith is a gift from our Heavenly Father. Both the Bible and Book of Mormon teach that faith is a gift of the Spirit, like the gift of tongues or healing (see 1 Corinthians 12:8–9; see also Moroni 10:8–11). Thus, like grace, in order for us to "have" faith, we must first receive it from the Lord. And then we must show gratitude for that gift by striving to increase our faith.

Because a divine gift is required, *we cannot simply discipline ourselves into heaven.* It is not by stubborn willpower but by the gift of "faith on the Lord Jesus Christ" that we can "withstand every temptation of the devil" (Alma 37:33). And "faith unto repentance" (Alma 34:16) is more than changing our actions (as if, on our own, we could even do that permanently). The Greek word for *repentance* used in the New Testament, *metanoia,* does not connote disciplined, sorrowful change in actions but—this is amazing—literally translates into "a transformative change of heart."[59] So true repentance involves faith—a gift—and a change of heart, another gift.

Performing good works without reliance on the Lord is not obedience, nor will it necessarily lead to faith. Well-intentioned works are not a precondition for faith, but instead a litmus test, an evidence, that it exists.[60] Paul confirmed this when he wrote, "For by grace are ye saved through faith; and that not of yourselves: it is the gift of God: Not of works, lest any man should boast" (Ephesians 2:8–9).

Jacob explained that the "Lord God showeth us our weakness that we may know that it is by his grace, and his great condescensions unto the children of men, that we have power to do these things" (Jacob 47). In other words, we are saved not by our own works, but by grace—the enabling power that helps us obey and repent. And that gift is received by the gift of faith.

We cannot boast that our own works are instrumental to either faith unto repentance or repentance unto salvation, because *works are not a precondition but a result of the grace that comes from the gift of faith.* Isaiah confirmed that it was God himself who "hast wrought all our works in us" (Isaiah 26:12). Even the Savior humbly explained that "the Father that dwelleth in me, *he doeth the works*" (John 14:10; emphasis added). Ultimately, it is by "grace that we are saved, after all we can do," and on our own we can do very little, particularly without humbly recognizing just how little that is (2 Nephi 25:23).[61]

To summarize, receiving the gift of a changed heart requires humility and faith in Christ. But faith, like a mighty change of heart, is a gift. It is not something we merely exercise on our own. Therefore we need one gift (faith) in order to receive the second gift (a mighty change), which raises a question: how do we get that first gift?

As is often the case, we need humility.

We Receive the Gift of Faith through Humility

In *The Articles of Faith,* Elder James E. Talmage explains what precedes the gift of faith: "Though within the reach of all who diligently strive to gain it, *faith is nevertheless a divine gift . . .* Although faith is called the first principle of the Gospel of Christ, though it be in fact the foundation of religious life, yet even *faith is preceded by sincerity of disposition* and *humility of soul,* whereby the word of God may make an impression upon the heart."[62]

We can't overstate the importance of humility. It is both one of two prerequisites for a change of heart, and a precedent to that second prerequisite, which is faith! The Lord's promise in Ether shows similar emphasis, repeating the word *humble* three times in order to teach how weak things are made strong (see Ether 12:27).

It is impossible to receive or maintain faith without humility. I've seen this with friends who have left the Church for "intellectual reasons," for example. With the Internet's glut of anti-Mormonism, there appears to be a growing trend toward leaving the Church on a so-called academic basis. Some struggle with faith when they read about alleged imperfections of early Church leaders—though earlier Church leaders in the Bible often illustrate even greater imperfections. Still, they place their trust in their own ideas about how a Church leader ought to be.

> Performing good works without reliance on the Lord is not obedience, nor will it necessarily lead to faith.

Some struggle with faith in the Book of Mormon when they hear arguments against its historicity, translation process, you name it. But this too is less rational than it appears. *There ought to be good arguments against the Book of Mormon's truthfulness.* In fact, we should expect numerous unresolved questions about

Lamanite DNA, where the events did or didn't take place, and every other evidentiary linchpin.

Imagine if there weren't real, solid reasons to question the Book of Mormon. What if someone found the proof? What if some archaeologist discovered Zarahemla, dug up wheels, horse bones, and scripture fragments in reformed Egyptian? What happens to our faith then? We'd have knowledge, but "faith is not to have a perfect knowledge" (Alma 32:21). *Faith requires room for doubt.* I can't help but believe this is all part of God's plan.

Just like we have "a God-given forgetfulness"[63] of our premortal existence, we must learn to walk by faith. Having evidentiary proof over doctrinal fundamentals would make faith impossible and devalue our mortal experience.

I also know people who have lost faith in the Church because certain practices or doctrines didn't match their own feelings—some held quite passionately—about how things "ought to be." This too is a symptom of pride. It takes humility to admit that you might be wrong about what the Church should or shouldn't do right now. Moreover, even if your beliefs are later validated (like statements/practices concerning blacks at certain points in Church history), you are not the prophet. By design, our perfect Church is governed by amazing but imperfect men. Through their ongoing revelation—not yours—changes will occur. And these changes will happen on God's time, not our own. But when you think about it, if changes didn't happen on God's time— which always seems to be later than some prefer—then they wouldn't try our faith!

Perhaps there are things you'd change if you were the prophet. Personally, I might make church two hours long instead of three. But then again, do you really want to belong to a church created by mortal convenience? I've been to those churches. There's one in Las Vegas that was completely designed by a survey. Starbucks in the lobby, popcorn in the pews, one secular rock song to kick things off—even the sermon subject matter was designed to give people what they wanted. How can anyone have faith in something they made up? It feels like idol worship.

Unless we humbly recognize that we don't understand everything but that we will follow the promptings of the Spirit nonetheless, we cannot have faith. President Boyd K. Packer explained that faith requires us to temporarily stop relying on our physical senses and "learn to walk to the edge of the light, and then a few steps into the darkness" because only "then the light will appear and show the way before you."[64]

This inability to rely on sources of earthly perception is described in Lehi's vision of the tree of life. To receive the love of God, which is the "most precious and most desirable," and "the greatest of all the gifts of God" (1 Nephi 15:36), we must follow a narrow path through mists of darkness which "blindeth the eyes" (1 Nephi 12:17). Only by humbly "holding fast" to His word can we receive this gift in this life or in the next (1 Nephi 8:30).

Thus, in our fallen state, mortal reasoning will not guide us to our desired destination. We cannot help ourselves. Heaven aside, our own understanding is not even sufficient to keep us on the path to peace or joy in this life. Accepting any precept of religion requires humble acceptance despite rational doubt. This is inevitable; pride and faith are like oil and water.

Humility also precedes faith because faith also requires an honest recognition of our reliance upon the Savior. One analogy for faith is a power plant on a river.[65] Like a power plant that has no power except what it receives from a river's energy, we lack power to overcome repetitive sin on our own. We require the Lord's enabling grace to give us power, which comes from that gift of faith.

Faith Sufficient for a Change of Heart Must Be Firm

As Mormon wrote, faith sufficient to precede a change of heart must be "firm" (Helaman 3:35). We need to want divine intervention with unwavering conviction. The explanation of this principle by the half brother of Christ brought Joseph Smith the First Vision. No man can even "think that he shall receive any thing of the Lord," wrote James, unless he "ask[s] in faith, nothing wavering. For he that wavereth is like a wave of the sea driven with the wind and tossed" (James 1:6–7). Joseph Smith later taught, "Where doubt is, there faith has no power."[66]

After all, if we don't really want the Lord to change our hearts and attitude toward temptation, why would He do it?

Nephi's words convey this sincere desire for a mighty change: "O Lord, wilt thou redeem my soul? Wilt thou deliver me out of the hands of mine enemies? *Wilt thou make me that I may shake at the appearance of sin?* May the gates of hell be shut continually before me, because that my heart is broken and my spirit is contrite!" (2 Nephi 4:31–32; emphasis added).

The Lord blesses us with a mighty change of heart—which includes "shak[ing] at the appearance of sin"[67]—only when we have strong humility and firm faith.

The righteousness of an entire civilization can be affected by unwavering faith. When the Lamanites became more righteous than the Nephites, for example, it was "because of their *firmness* and their *steadiness in the faith*" (Helaman 6:1; emphasis added).

Lamoni's father, the Lamanite king, is another powerful example of firm faith found in the Book of Mormon. When Aaron, one of the sons of Mosiah (who had a mighty change of heart himself) taught the king about God, the plan of redemption, and the Atonement, this Lamanite king longed to receive those blessings. His commitment to rely upon the Lord was so firm that he exclaimed "I will give up all that I possess, yea, I will forsake my kingdom, that I may receive this great joy" (Alma 22:15). Then—because even an entire kingdom is not enough—in prayer he told the Lord, "I will give away all my sins to know thee" (v. 18).

It is not surprising that, like his son Lamoni, the king was physically overcome by the Spirit and granted a mighty change of heart. Moreover, as with everyone who experiences this change, miracles followed. After the king had risen, he bore his testimony, converting "his whole household" (Alma 22:23). The king later helped missionaries (who had also previously received mighty changes of heart) bring thousands to the Lord by permitting them to teach without any opposition (see Alma 23:1–6).

> Too often, we know our commitment to change is halfhearted and wavering. And "wavering" faith will not suffice.

Perhaps some of us feel that we cannot attain a level of dedication similar to the Lamanite king. When stuck in a cycle of repeated sins—of commission or omission—it can seem impossible to have firm faith. Perhaps the first, second, or third time you tried to repent, you at least thought that you were exercising faith unto repentance. You wanted to change, and yet your faith faltered. Perhaps you wanted to give up a lot of your sins. But unlike Lamoni's father, you were not ready to forsake all. Then, when you later relapsed, it got even harder to trust your ability to permanently change. *Too often, we know our commitment to change is halfhearted and wavering. And "wavering" faith will not suffice.*

What if we want to have firm faith, but don't have it? Should we abandon hope?

No. Remember: the gift of faith is also preceded by sincere desire. We just need to *really* want it.

KEY POINTS

FIRM FAITH

1. We only receive the gift of a mighty change of heart after having first received the gift of firm faith.

2. Firm faith constitutes trusting the Savior. We should trust the Savior more than our own flawed understanding. We can't focus solely on our own ability to obey because that is relying on an "arm of flesh" and leads to pride.

3. Firm faith is not something you do, but a gift you receive. Scriptures clarify that this gift is preceded by humble trust in the Lord and a sincere desire.

4. Faith cannot be received or maintained without humility.

5. Firm faith is unwavering.

CHAPTER 6

SINCERE DESIRE—
YOU HAVE TO WANT IT

*If you will here stop and ask yourself, why you
are not as pious as the primitive Christians were, your
own heart will tell you, that it is neither through
ignorance nor inability, but purely because you
never thoroughly intended it.*

WILLIAM LAW[68]

Too often, we live beneath our capacity to excel. We dwell in realms of mediocrity because, quite frankly, trying hard is hard. We also fail to reach our true potential because we rarely decide what we actually want to achieve. As Charles de Gaulle explained, "Nothing great will ever be achieved without great men, and men are great only if they are determined to be so."[69]

This brings us to the other precursor to the gift of faith. Along with being filled with humility, there is a second condition referred to as a "sincerity of disposition."[70] Moroni describes this as having "a sincere heart" and "real intent" (Moroni 10:4). As is often the case with our merciful Lord, the focus is upon our desire, not our alleged ability. Remember, King Benjamin did not say that we must be "*able* to submit" to the Lord's divine will; we must be "*willing* to submit" (Mosiah 3:19; emphasis added).

Those who were baptized at the Waters of Mormon covenanted to be "*willing* to bear one another's burdens" and "*willing* to mourn with those that mourn" (Mosiah 18:8–9; emphasis

73

added). Our blessing on the sacrament bread (the only one that mentions commandments) similarly asks that we be "*willing* to take upon [us] the name of [the] Son, and always remember him and keep his commandments" (Moses 4:3).

After the Savior instituted the sacrament among the Nephites, He again emphasized the desire or willingness to obey, as opposed to achieving perfect obedience. "Blessed are ye for this thing which ye have done, for this is fulfilling my commandments," He said, "and this doth witness unto the Father that ye are *willing* to do that which I have commanded you" (3 Nephi 18:10; emphasis added). This focus on our will or desire is fundamental.

If we were required to fully "keep the commandments" in order to have the Holy Spirit's presence, we would break that covenant within minutes of making it. We would almost never be worthy of feeling the Spirit. But when we realize that our commitment is to be *willing* to keep the commandments—when what is required is "sincerity of disposition"—we *can* receive His comfort. We can receive His enabling strength. Of course we must always repent (immediately and often, as will be discussed in chapter 8), but this too demonstrates our humble heart, our sincere desire, our willingness to follow Him.

In short, you have to want it. You must decide that from now on you do not want to rely on your own flawed mortal reasoning and physical inclinations (i.e., the arm of flesh). You must definitively want those sins you have enjoyed to become unacceptable and not even desirable. You must want to follow His will in everything.

This decision encompasses relying upon His plans, which may not mirror our own short-sighted dreams. As Elder Hugh B. Brown said, "You sometimes wonder whether the Lord really knows what he ought to do with you. You sometimes wonder if you know better than he does about what you ought to do and ought to become."[71] Like Alma with his dream of being an angel (see Alma 29:1–6), to have a mighty change of heart, you need to accept that the Lord does know best.

Elder Brown told a classic story about a currant bush that grew too high, turned to wood, and had no blossoms or fruit. After the gardener pruned the bush until it was nothing but a "little clump of stumps," the bush (metaphorically) cried, upset at not becoming a tall shade or fruit tree.[72]

Like the pruned currant bush, we too have ideas about what we should do or become. The gardener said to the bush, "'Look, little currant bush, I am the gardener here, and I know what I want you to be. I didn't intend you to be a fruit tree or a shade tree. I want you to be a currant bush, and some day, little currant bush, when you are laden with fruit, you are going to say, "Thank you, Mr. Gardener, for loving me enough to cut me down, for caring enough about me to hurt me."'"

Elder Brown concluded, "I just want you to know that if you don't get what you think you ought to get, remember, God is the gardener here. He knows what he wants you to be."[73] Moreover, *He knows what* you *want you to be.* He knows who you truly are.

You Must Make a True Decision

One obstacle to surrendering to the Lord's will is that we are not accustomed to making actual decisions. The Latin roots for the word *decision* are *de* ("from") and *caedere* ("to cut"). A decision permanently "cuts off" every future course of action but one. There is no changing courses; there is no going back.

Too often, like folding down a page in a *Choose Your Own Adventure* book so that you can backtrack if you need to, we make halfhearted choices, assuming we can just turn back and take a different path if the going gets tough. Maybe you can do that with a book, but not with life. Life is not a *Choose Your Own Adventure* story, and noncommittal choices are not decisions. Nor will they serve you well. Only when you've made a true decision—when you've cut off all the other options—will you have the strength to persevere through the obstacles that inevitably lie ahead.

As a missionary, I had many opportunities to teach a program designed to help people stop smoking. Over time, a pattern emerged. I began to see a feature that distinguished those who quit from those who fell back into addiction.

First, everyone who started this program seemed determined to quit smoking. I saw mothers cry and promise their children that they were done filling the trailer with secondhand smoke. I saw men tell everyone in their lives to never give them a cigarette if they asked. People bought bags full of hard cinnamon candies, gallons of orange juice, and posted reminder notes around their homes and offices. From an outsider's perspective, every person who joined this program wanted to change.

All of the steps provided were usually followed except one. Whenever somebody fell back to smoking again, my companion and I asked them where he or she got the first cigarette. Inevitably, the answer went something like this: "Just in case, I kept a few cigarettes in my sock drawer." *When you make a true decision—when you "cut off" all other options—you don't leave cigarettes in your sock drawer.*

In other words, if part of you hangs on to the possibility of repeating any sinful behavior, you didn't really decide! The Lord is not going to remove your desire for sin if you don't want it. *He is not going to help you rely solely on Him if you'd rather keep one foot in Babylon.* The Lord will go above and beyond to help us, but if we don't exercise our agency to at least *firmly decide* what we want, He cannot give it to us.

Elder Jeffrey R. Holland stated this concept perfectly: "You can change anything you want to change, and you can do it very fast. That's another satanic suckerpunch—that it takes years and years and eons of eternity to repent. It takes exactly as long to repent as it takes you to say, 'I'll change'—*and mean it.* . . . You may well spend—indeed you had better spend—the rest of your life proving your repentance by its permanence. But change, growth, renewal, and repentance can come for you as instantaneously as for Alma and the sons of Mosiah."[74]

This instantaneous change requires decisiveness. We cannot commit halfheartedly. Only when we "love God with all [our] might, mind and strength, then is his grace sufficient for [us]" (Moroni 10:32).

> When you make a true decision—when you "cut off" all other options—you don't leave cigarettes in your sock drawer.

Let's take this one step further. What if you want to have that resolve, that decisiveness to follow Him, but you are so stuck in your habitual cycles, so wavering in your faith, that you still need help? What if all you have is a desire to believe, but that desire is so weak that you still can't help but put a couple of proverbial cigarettes into your sock drawer?

What then? Fortunately, our Savior's "arm of mercy is [always] extended towards [us], and whosoever will come, him will [He] receive" (3 Nephi 9:14).

All We Need Is One Particle of Honest Desire for God's Help

The Apostle Mark tells of Jesus casting out a demon from a child (see Mark 9:17–27). This evil spirit was so strong that the other disciples were not able to cast it out. The child foamed and gnashed his teeth, and the spirit even "cast [the boy] into the fire, and into the waters, to destroy him" (Mark 9:22).

Jesus told the child's father "all things are possible to him that believeth" (Mark 9:23). If ever a father wanted faith sufficient to the miracle, it was this father. But he was also honest in this crucial moment. He knew that his faith might not be enough. The father "cried out, and said with tears, Lord, I believe; help thou mine unbelief" (v. 24). Regardless of the insufficient level of his faith, his desire was sincere. And on that basis, Jesus immediately cast out the evil spirit (see vv. 25–27).

We Must Be Totally Honest with the Lord

"So I kneeled down. But the words wouldn't come. Why wouldn't they? It warn't no use to try and hide it from Him. Nor from ME, neither. I knowed very well why they wouldn't come. It was because my heart warn't right; it was because I warn't square; it was because I was playing double. I was letting ON to give up sin, but away inside of me I was holding on to the biggest one of all. I was trying to make my mouth SAY I would do the right thing . . . but deep down in me I knowed it was a lie, and He knowed it. You can't pray a lie—I found that out."

—Huck Finn[75]

Oliver Cowdery was granted a knowledge of anything he asked in faith "with an honest heart" (D&C 8:1). Nephi spoke of having "full purpose of heart" and no "hypocrisy" or "deception" before God (2 Nephi 31:13). Honesty with the Lord is essential.

Consequently, the suggestion that we should hide our sins is one of Satan's most persuasive tactics. Remember, it was the "father of lies" who taught secrecy to the Gadianton robbers (see Helaman 6:16–32), and it was those "secret combinations" that caused the destruction of the Nephite and Jaredite nations (see Ether 8:15–26; see also Helaman 2:12–13).

The first mistake Adam and Eve made after eating the forbidden fruit was to try and "hide themselves from the presence of the Lord" (Moses 4:14). Even in God's presence, our progenitors tried to keep their transgression a secret. This is a detrimental mortal inclination.

Satan wants us to think that if nobody knows our sin, everything is fine. Where I live, that suggestion is promoted daily. Our town is known as Sin City, and our $75,000,000 ad campaign[76] from 2005 was everywhere: "What happens in Vegas stays in Vegas." As if you could "sin it up," go home, and face no consequences because nobody will be the wiser.

Satan wants us to believe we can (and should) keep one foot in Babylon and the other in Zion because, after all, everybody sins. He wants us to believe we can serve two masters, but that is impossible.

> The Lord is not going to help you rely solely on Him if you'd rather keep one foot in Babylon.

In the entertainment business, I've met countless people who live double lives. For example, I know one record label executive who maintained two families and an additional mistress without any of them discovering his duplicity (triplicity?) for years. In the end, however, he could never be fast enough to outrun the mounting lies required to hide repetitive sin.[77]

Attempting to serve two masters requires "a lying tongue, and . . . A false witness that speaketh lies"—two things that "the Lord hate[s]" (Proverbs 6:16–19). The Lord *hates* lying. Why does the Lord hate secrecy and lying so badly?

First, lying to others is often accompanied by lying to ourselves and, ultimately, believing those lies. Some of us rationalize that a repeated sin is unavoidable due to personal weaknesses and inclinations. It would be "unnatural" to restrain your carnal inclinations, says the natural man.

Many of us also rationalize that our repeated sins are ultimately inconsequential. Even denominations with good intentions teach that God will "justify in committing a little sin; . . . there is no harm in this; . . . and at last we shall be saved in the kingdom of God" (2 Nephi 28:7–12). But this too is a lie. Repetitive sin is absolutely consequential because it hardens hearts, decreases our ability to repent, and makes us "past feeling" the Holy Spirit's vital presence. Indeed, "when we undertake to cover our sins, . . . the Spirit of the Lord is grieved" and ultimately "withdrawn" (D&C 121:37).

Moreover, lying to God is ignorant, because it is impossible. God is all knowing and omnipresent. Of course, He "knowest thy thoughts and the intents of thy heart" (D&C 6:16). As President Spencer W. Kimball put it, "There are no corners so dark, no deserts so uninhabited, no canyons so remote, no automobiles so hidden, no homes so tight and shut in but that the all-seeing One can penetrate and observe."[78]

Regardless of our forms of transgression or insufficient faith, there is no point in trying to hide from the Lord and everything to gain by being honest with Him. We should not hesitate to reveal our beliefs and desires to our loving Father. After all, God already knows our heart. "There lives more faith in honest doubt, believe me, than in half the creeds," wrote Tennyson.[79]

As the father of the child possessed by a demon discovered, Christ can help our unbelief and work miracles when we are honest about our doubts. Some years ago, my mom lost the diamond in her engagement ring and was distraught. She believed God cared about her concern, but she didn't have faith that she could hear God well enough to find the lost item. She prayerfully apologized for not being able to hear His voice and humbly asked if He could help her feel. Soon thereafter, she walked into the laundry room barefoot and stepped on the diamond.

Whether you are struggling with faith or uncertain who you really want to be and what you really want to do, there is no reason to hide from God. "Wrestle" with him, if you need to (Enos 1:2). At whatever stage you are in, He already knows the desires of your heart and will help you, as long as you are honest with Him and with yourself. *If you aren't ready to fully trust God, admit it. And when you are ready to trust your all-powerful, all-knowing, loving Father, tell Him.*

We Need to Decide if We Really Want a Change of Heart

While attending NYU Law School, I passed two homeless girls in the West Village. When one asked for money to buy food, I bought them hamburgers and fries. As we ate, they told me about their life on the street.

Their stories were heartbreaking. Beneath multiple piercings, tattoos, and filthy clothes, I saw two sad and lonely young women in their early twenties. They described the dangers of sleeping in parks, being robbed on the street, and bad experiences they'd had in homeless shelters.

"What do you girls need, then?" I asked.

They said sixty dollars would be enough to eat and get a room in a cheap motel.

My heart went out to them. "So if I found you on this corner and gave you sixty dollars every day, would you be happy?"

After a moment of silence, the younger of the two began to cry and then shook her head.

"How can I help, then?" I asked.

"We want jobs," the other one explained. Without résumés or

clean clothes, the places they had approached were unwilling to hire them. I took their cell phone number and volunteered to help.

I first found a customer service job and reached out to the girls. We met again on that street corner, and they told me that they didn't want secretarial or phone work. They also didn't want jobs in two different places. What they really wanted were waitressing jobs at the same restaurant. This felt a bit choosy, but they seemed sincere. So, again, I went through local help-wanted advertisements and made phone calls.

I found a kind man who agreed to give the two young women work uniforms and a job waiting tables in a Russian restaurant. Sight unseen, he extended this opportunity solely because he agreed that these two homeless girls just needed a chance.

When I told the girls, they broke down. They were so appreciative, so excited. I gave them the address, start date, and time. They agreed that the location and hours were perfect. I felt wonderful.

Unfortunately, that feeling didn't last. On day one, they didn't show up for work. I convinced their employer to give them another chance. When I reached them, they gave me a story about being stuck in Brooklyn having to "watch a friend's house." I said they had another chance to work the following day, but if they didn't show up they would lose the job. They apologized profusely and thanked me, swearing they would be there.

Again, they didn't show.

When I called them, frustrated, I got another poor excuse. After once more speaking with the owner, I told them they could go to work any day they wanted and that he would give them a chance. I also said that I wouldn't keep following up. If they really wanted that job, it was theirs.

Weeks later, I ran into the same girls begging on the street. As it turned out, they had never shown up to the restaurant. I thought about giving them a hard time, but then I realized it wasn't worth it.

These girls had hard lives and obviously needed help. Their claims to want help seemed sincere. But, in the end, their desires were not sincere enough. They only *thought* they wanted something I could offer. They liked the idea of a stable job, but they never honestly decided to take one.

Like those two destitute young women, if we aren't certain we want help, God cannot help us. Only when we are truly honest—with a "full purpose of heart" and no "hypocrisy" or "deception before God" (2 Nephi 31:13)—is the Lord willing and able to grant a mighty change of heart.

> If you aren't ready to fully trust God, admit it. And when you are ready to trust your all-powerful, all-knowing, loving Father, tell Him.

In Alma's experiment with a proverbial seed, he explained that we need only to "exercise a particle of faith"—a particle as small as a sincere "desire to believe"—for the Lord to help us (Alma 32:27). We then need to "let this desire work in [us]," and because that seed of desire is good—as long as we nourish it and don't cast it out—it will grow (Alma 32:27). We do not need full-blown faith right out of the gates. Like the father of that possessed and suicidal son in the Bible, what we need is an honest "desire to believe." We need a sincere disposition. *When sincerity is combined with strong humility, the Lord gives us more desire and faith.*

Again, the role of works is secondary. Note the type of tree that Alma's seed becomes: the "tree of life" (Alma 32:40). This seed of honest desire grows into that same iconic tree dreamed of by Lehi and Nephi. The fruit of that tree is God's love. And the pure love of Christ is charity, which produces good works. We don't do good works and then receive faith, and we don't save ourselves. If we humbly and sincerely desire to believe, the Lord will help our unbelief, give us faith unto repentance, and fill us with His love. When we are full of charity, good works inevitably follow.

So, when you look at it, *the Lord gives us what we want!* God "granteth unto men according to their desire" (Alma 29:4). Even the sons of perdition receive what they want (see D&C 88:32).[80] Indeed, all of us will "enjoy that which [we] are willing [i.e., want] to receive." The "best gifts" are "given for the benefit of those who love [God] and keep all [His] commandments, and *him that seeketh so to do*" (D&C 46:8–9, emphasis added). We just need to decide if we really do want Him to intervene in our lives and help make our desires righteous.

We need the initial desire to let the Lord help. Given our moral agency, desire is not something that can be developed against our will. We need to want permanent change or the Lord will not intervene. Specifically, we need to want Him to not merely change our ability to overcome temptation but to change our very disposition. *We need to want Him to change our wants, to change our desires.* We must sincerely want our desire for those "sins we enjoy" to leave forever, without any doubt or hesitation.

We must decisively want a mighty change of heart, because when we are stuck in cycles of sin there is no other escape. We cannot forsake those sins alone by mere force of will, or we would have done so already.

Again, as Elder Bednar explains, this change is "not simply the result of working harder or developing greater individual discipline. Rather, it is the consequence of a fundamental change in our desires, our motives, and our natures made possible through the Atonement of Christ the Lord."[81] With the great Mediator's

Atonement and spiritual intervention, we may overcome "*both sin and the desire to sin,* both the taint and the tyranny of sin."[82]

Why did it take me so many years to realize this?

After graduating from seminary and studying for a year at BYU, I thought I understood the Atonement. I didn't question that until I was a new missionary, lying in bed and trying to fall asleep.

"I just don't understand," my senior companion said under his breath. It was late, and I was tired. "I just don't understand," he said again. Eyes closed, I wished he would stop talking and go to sleep. After he repeated this again, however, I couldn't help it.

"What don't you understand?"

"The Atonement," he replied. "I just don't understand it."

Well, this missionary was about to go home after two years of service, and I had yet to wear out a single pair of socks. But I was a little bothered by this late-night presentation, and I took the bait.

"What don't you understand?"

"How it works."

"What do you mean?"

"How it was possible, you know."

I remember trying to keep my mouth closed and trying to sleep, but I was curious about what this elder didn't understand. Certainly I'd heard some of the Brethren say there were things about the Atonement that they didn't understand. But I didn't know exactly what those things were. I didn't *know* what I didn't know, so to speak. I also felt like this elder was trying to put on a show.

"What, you think you understand how it was possible?" he asked after I remained silent.

I couldn't help myself. "I don't know, I think so. Christ was able to take upon Himself our sins and be resurrected by volunteering to put the Father's plan into operation in the premortal existence and living without sin. He had to have a mortal mother

(Mary), so He could experience temptation and die, and a divine Father (Heavenly Father), so He could be sinless and resurrected."

"You don't understand," my companion said.

"What don't I understand?" I asked, frustrated.

"You just don't understand."

Wound up, it took hours before I finally slept. I'm sorry to admit that I carried that frustration with me throughout my months with this companion. And I've thought about that incident many times since.

I now realize there are indeed many things I don't know about the Atonement (including still not knowing what it is I don't know). More importantly, I have since learned significant components to the Atonement that I did not understand while serving a mission. It's embarrassing how little I knew compared to that confidence I once displayed.

I did not understand that grace was something I needed in order to obey, as opposed to just some "difference" Christ made up after I died. I did not realize that the Atonement wasn't intended for me to simply repent over and over for the same sins but instead to remove my very desire to commit sin. For example, the Atonement doesn't only forgive someone for adultery; it can remove lust from his or her heart. Of course, I had read about mighty changes of heart. But for some reason I didn't realize they applied to me. I suspect I am not alone when it comes to an incomplete understanding.

In this life, we all need to have our hearts changed—gradually or mightily, and most likely repeatedly. The first step in receiving this vital blessing from the Atonement is to decisively want it.

Doing Something Just Because You "Think You Should" Is Not Enough

This is among the most productive inspiration I've ever received: just "doing what you think you should" doesn't cut it. It took way too many years for me to figure this out. When we are acting from external pressure—shame from not taking (or passing) the sacrament, not getting into BYU (or getting kicked out), delaying a mission or temple marriage, disappointing our parents or spouse, not wanting to confess something to our bishop, or alternatively "doing good" from positive peer pressure alone—we are being "acted upon" and not acting (2 Nephi 2:26). And the Lord sent us here to act.

Remember Satan's premortal plan: restrain agency so people have no choice to obey (see Moses 4:3). Satan is still pushing that devious proposal. Even the most well-intentioned parents, spouses, and leaders who use unrighteous manipulation and coercion[83] to elicit obedience are reading Satan's playbook! Ironically, the consequences of sin and manipulation are identical—restrained agency. In both cases, spiritual growth is stunted.

> If you are struggling with any temptation, you should ask yourself, what do I really want?

The Lord is not concerned with what we think we are *supposed* to want. He cares about what we actually *do* want. We are granted the actual desires of our heart. It's as simple as that. *If you are struggling with any temptation, you should ask yourself, what do I really want?* This is what matters. Be honest.

Be Aware of Those "Should" Versus "Want" Moments

If you said, for example, "I want to smoke pot right now, but I know I shouldn't," an alarm should go off in your head. Immediately stop and take time to decide what you really want.[84] Don't just think about what you are supposed to do; that isn't good enough. "Should" versus "want" moments are critical.

In these crossroads, you need to discover not what you

"should" do (which is usually obvious) but what you honestly want. And, as Elder Maxwell put it, you also had "better want the consequences of what you want!"[85] You might enjoy the euphoria you get from a high—we all like to feel good—but do you want to break the law, risk incarceration, lose control, become paranoid, do something you'll regret, harm another person, have a bad trip, have a bad hangover, or become one step closer to addiction? These are actual, statistically probable consequences.

So take time to explore the possible repercussions. Imagine the long-term effects of your action (or inaction)—all of them. *Uncertainty over what we want to do (and the struggle of "should" versus "want") often occurs when we are not realistically considering all of the possible consequences.*

Like some sneaky supervillain, sometimes we think we can avoid natural law. Perhaps we took steps to ensure certain negative effects of sin did not occur. An unwanted pregnancy didn't happen; those you neglected to visit teach appear to be doing fine; the drinks or pornography or recreational drugs haven't caused an addiction—not yet, at least. Occasionally, when lying to ourselves and others, it may seem as if we have avoided all of a sin's negative consequences—all except for losing the Holy Spirit, of course (which perhaps we barely noticed, due to a hardened heart).

However, aside from losing blessings from the Holy Spirit's presence, there is another problem: as the Apostle Paul put it, *we might "enjoy the pleasures of sin for a season," but every season ends* (Hebrews 11:25). I have a picture of myself touching the tail of an enormous alligator on a golf course. As anyone who sees that picture reminds me, getting so close was not smart. Although we might occasionally pet spiritual crocodiles without obvious harm, someday we will get bitten. Thinking we can "get away" without negative effects also develops unreasonably high tolerance for spiritual risk. The devil's "flatter[y]" that we are sneaky supervillains—that we can indefinitely avoid the consequences of sin—is a lie. He is "cheat[ing our] souls" and "lull[ing us] away into carnal security" (2 Nephi 28:21–22). As the saying goes, "there are old mushroom hunters and there are bold mushroom hunters, but there are no old, bold mushroom hunters."[86]

Every sin has negative effects in your life and in the lives of others. And there's more. Your choices don't only impact external events; they impact who you are. What type of man or woman do you want to be? How do such men and women act? What do they do?

Remember, you can do what you want, and you can be who and what you want to be. If you are sincere, with a mighty change of heart, the Lord can change your very disposition.

Inspired Bishops, Therapists, Friends, and Family Can Help

Sometimes talking with others can help you recognize your honest desires. Ecclesiastical leaders and counselors or therapists (individually or in a twelve-step program) are often inspired and well trained to help you determine what you really want. And from time to time, we can all use another set of eyes to evaluate the consequences of our behavior. Another perspective can help you balance long-term desires against short-term actions—guilt-laden, endorphin-seeking behavior against honesty and peace. Do not shy away from smart and inspired counseling. There is nothing wrong, and a lot right, with getting help.

A friend of mine, Todd, recently finished the Spartan race—a nine-mile obstacle course designed to make your entire body hurt. At one point, Todd came to a pit of water that he had to cross using an overhead beam and swinging ropes. Anyone who fell into the water had to do thirty "burpees" (a hybrid of planks, jumping, and pushups). The obstacle was nearly insurmountable, especially after already completing over half of the grueling race. Todd did not want to do those burpees. Right before him, however, he saw a couple taking turns carrying each other back and forth across the water—totally legal, no burpees! However, Todd had entered this race alone; he didn't have a partner. He wanted to use that couple's strategy, but, like most guys on a nine-mile manhood exhibition, perhaps, Todd felt embarrassed asking a stranger for help. So he gave it a shot alone, fell in the water, and miserably had to do the thirty burpees. Never be ashamed to ask for help. From time to time, we all need it.

> We might "enjoy the pleasures of sin for a season," but every season ends.

Moreover, when the Spirit bears witness of what you hear from that inspired friend or counselor, you can be reminded of the path that, in your heart, you know you want. You can remember not just who you "should" be, but who you truly are.

In conclusion, don't let the devil tell you that you can't do what you want because of parents or Church or spouses or anyone. You can do whatever you want. You have moral agency. This is your life, and you ought to do what you want. But here's the kicker: when you honestly consider everything and allow the Spirit to help you make decisions, guess what? You will find that your desires are right in line with the will of a loving Heavenly Father.

There is no reason for rebelliousness. And when you accept this truth—this blessing granted by the Lord's plan and sacrifice of His Son—you will experience true freedom. You can act instead of be acted upon and grow into the spiritual giant you truly are but never realized you could be.

Firm Faith Requires Prayerfully Asking God without Hypocrisy or Deception

Prayer with "full purpose of heart" and no "hypocrisy" or "deception" before God is essential to receiving firm faith (2 Nephi 31:13). Such sincere prayer, as demonstrated by Enos, Nephi, and others, can be intense. It can require extreme focus and concentration. However it transpires, when you petition the Lord with that honest desire, His word—His iron rod—will guide you through the darkness.

Faith moves mountains that are not always physical. Getting a spouse to trust and forgive you after you've betrayed his or her trust can be a mountain. Overcoming addiction can be a mountain. Making permanent changes in areas where we have repeatedly failed can be mountains. But God moves mountains. He "give[s] liberally to him that asketh" (2 Ne. 4:35).

If we ask for bread, He will not give us a stone; if we ask for a fish, He will not give us a serpent; if we ask for an egg, He will not give us a scorpion (see Luke 11:11–13). He loves us, regardless of our weaknesses. In fact, *He gave us those weaknesses.* He placed us in a world with mortal limitations so we can be humble and turn to Him, because we cannot escape our cycles of sin alone.

The Lord will "surely . . . redeem his people, but he should not come to redeem them in their sins, *but to redeem them* from their sins" (Helaman 5:10; emphasis added). He wants to change our attitude toward temptation. He wants to change our desires, our very dispositions. Whether gradually or instantaneously, we can and must obtain a change of heart. It is a covenant responsibility,[20] and it will bring our greatest joy and peace. All we need to do is *want it.* Honestly. And then *ask for it.*

This is the good news.

KEY POINTS

SINCERE DESIRE

1. Mighty changes of heart are granted when we truly want them and humbly ask in faith for the Lord to intervene in our lives.

2. When we are struggling with temptation—or when we find ourselves torn between what we think we *should* do and what we think we *want* to do—we should pause, accept our God-given agency, and ask ourselves what we really want.

3. In the end, the Lord gives us what we want. He will grant us the honest desires of our hearts.

PART THREE

"CAN YE FEEL SO NOW?"

HOW TO MAINTAIN A MIGHTY CHANGE OF HEART

CHAPTER 7

NO MORE DISPOSITION
TO DO EVIL

Teach them to withstand every temptation of the devil,
with their faith on the Lord Jesus Christ.

ALMA 37:33

A round 83 BC, Alma asked his brethren: "If ye have experienced a change of heart, and if ye have felt to sing the song of redeeming love, I would ask, *can ye feel so now?*" (Alma 5:26; emphasis added). This is what the Nephites needed to hear. Despite the mighty change and miracles they had received, they repeatedly failed to protect their spiritual hearts from rehardening.

Like the Nephites, we have that same tendency to be "quick to forget." Despite the miracles we have undeniably received, we too are inclined to soon thereafter let our hearts grow hard. Part 3 of this book is devoted to Alma's challenge to "feel so now"— maintaining the results of that mighty change of heart.

Scriptural accounts of a mighty change of heart are useful for those who seek that change as well as those who want to continue "feel[ing] so now." We repeatedly learn that the results of a mighty change include (1) "hav[ing] no more disposition to do evil" and (2) "do[ing] good continually" (Mosiah 5:2). Both phrases have significance.

This chapter discusses our change in disposition to no more do evil. The next chapter will cover doing good continually.

A Disposition That Shakes at the Appearance of Sin

Disposition is defined as "a person's inherent qualities of mind and character."[87] Synonyms include *nature, character,* and *mentality*.[88] Losing your "disposition to do evil" does not mean you have an increased ability to overcome temptation. Instead, losing a disposition to do evil actually changes what you find tempting. It changes your very nature and appetite for sin.[89]

As one BYU professor explained: "Our desires come and go, often in relation to our environment, but character and personality are more permanent, more fundamental to the makeup of our soul. The change of heart we seek that accompanies true repentance actually brings a change of appetite for sin. Our likes and dislikes relative to good and evil are shaped by the Atonement. We learn not only to avoid the sin but the temptation to sin as well. There is no earthly entity that has this power to change our temperament. Wars are fought trying to bend people's wills and loyalties, but only the Savior can transform within us something so fundamental as our character and our appetites."[90]

> Losing a disposition to do evil actually changes what you find tempting.

The Savior demonstrated His disposition toward sin and temptation when the devil tempted Him in the wilderness (see Matthew 4:1–10). Christ could have allowed the devil to keep following Him around tempting Him, all the while remaining sinless. But He didn't. Instead, He said, "Get thee hence, Satan," commanding Satan and his persuasive lures to get out of there (Matthew 4:10). *Christ didn't continue to oppose temptation; He ordered it to leave.* We need to want and maintain this same dispositional change.

Nephi (son of Lehi) sought a permanent change, hoping to become more like the Lord, unable to "look upon sin with the least degree of allowance" (D&C 1:31). After lamenting his struggles with temptation, Nephi implored the Lord: "Wilt thou make me that I may shake at the appearance of sin? May the gates of hell be shut continually before me, because that my heart is broken and my spirit is contrite!" (2 Nephi 4:31–32).

Of course Nephi was not praying to be afraid of any person or thing that had the appearance of sin. Instead, Nephi wanted to shake the moment sin appeared, or at the first sign of temptation. This humble response requires recognizing our own weaknesses so clearly that we feel appropriate danger when enticing sins are near.

> Christ didn't continue to oppose temptation; He ordered it to leave.

I have wondered about my own desire to "shake" the instant temptations arise. How often have I allowed myself to get close to sin without intending to get burned? How often do we all push the boundaries of morality or the Word of Wisdom while expecting to remain obedient? Misjudging our own strength to withstand temptation is like the proverbial frog growing accustomed to a pot of boiling water. As long as the water temperature rises slowly, the frog will die before jumping out.[91] We'd like to think we are smart and capable enough to push sin's boundary and escape unscathed, but we are not.

Avoid Proximity to Enticing Sins and Escape Temptation at the Earliest Moment

"A good man's got to know his limitations."

—CLINT EASTWOOD (DIRTY HARRY IN *MAGNUM FORCE*)

After a change of heart, we cannot be casual about encountering temptations that were once enticing. Instead, our disposition toward spiritual threats is (and should remain) a healthy fear. Elder F. Enzio Busche counseled that we ought to "avoid any fear like your worst enemy, but magnify your fear about the consequences of sin."[92] President Packer suggested we view temptation like spiritual crocodiles, capable of leaping from hiding places and "bit[ing] you to pieces." Worse than any physical animal, however, "spiritual crocodiles can kill or mutilate your souls."[93]

As with crocodiles, we need to remember that the most dangerous temptations are those lurking nearby. Lot learned this the hard way when he and his uncle Abram (before he became Abraham) chose new lands for their cattle. The people of Sodom were "wicked and sinners," but the land was fertile (Genesis 13:10, 13). So, unlike Abram, Lot "pitched his tent towards Sodom" (v. 12). This proximity led to Lot later moving to Sodom, being taken captive, risking the safety of his daughters, and ultimately losing his wife (who looked back to Sodom, wishing to return, and turned into a pillar of salt).

With healthy caution, those who have experienced (or seek to experience) a change of heart take every reasonable step to avoid getting close to what they find tempting. I recently went to a morning service at a very old church in Wales that my ancestors had attended. As the pastor read the Lord's Prayer, I was struck by the following: "Lead us not into temptation, but deliver us from evil" (Matthew 6:13). We know God does not tempt man (see James 1:13). So what does this mean?

I think the Savior is asking us to pray for help not only to avoid sin but to avoid the very temptation of sin. Matthew 26:41 seems to make this even clearer: "Watch and pray, that ye enter not into temptation: the spirit indeed is willing, but the flesh is weak." For me, the key word is *watch*. What are we watching for, if not for temptation? We aren't just to overcome temptation when it is present—we are to avoid it. We are to pray and watch out for it so that we can escape *before* we find our flesh too weak. Indeed, we must "watch and pray continually, that [we] may not be tempted above that which [we] can bear" (Alma 13:28). We each have "favorite sins" that cannot be avoided by willpower alone; we must avoid the corresponding temptation altogether.

In Alma 31:10, we learn that the prideful Zoramites (in a warning to our day) did not follow the Lord's Prayer: "Neither would they observe the performances of the church, to continue in prayer and supplication to God daily, that they might not enter into temptation."

Pride lets us think we can stand in fire without getting burned. We think we are strong enough to fight temptation, when we ought to be asking for God's help in avoiding it altogether. Praying to not even enter into temptation is a crucial step in developing no more disposition to do evil—after all, if we keep ourselves far out of reach of the sin, how can it stand a chance of enticing us?

> It takes great humility to recognize you cannot even get close to those sins you find most tempting.

We each know well which sins pose the greatest danger for us. Thus, we must continually keep a wide berth. For a recovering alcoholic, this often means avoiding bars and former drinking buddies. For the people of Anti-Nephi-Lehi, this meant eliminating every opportunity for bloodshed, even removing their ability to defend themselves. King Anti-Nephi-Lehi described this people as "the most lost of all mankind" because of all their "sins and the many murders which [they had] committed" (Alma 24:11). Murder was, for them, an enticing sin. Thus, after feeling God's mercy, they buried their swords to keep that temptation at bay (see Alma 24:15).[94] *It takes great humility to recognize you cannot even get close to those sins you find most tempting.*

In addition to avoiding proximity to sin, those who have experienced mighty changes of heart find a way to escape tempting situations immediately. For example, when another man's wife tried to seduce Joseph of Egypt, he ran out of the room so fast that he left his "garment in her hand" (Genesis 39:12).

I have more than once misinterpreted this story as I've narrowly escaped various transgressions. I've congratulated myself for leaving the situation at one of the last possible moments. That attitude is wrong and dangerous.

In an eternal scheme, each decision we make to linger near sin is like petting that spiritual crocodile. Joseph ran from Potiphar's wife as soon as she was clutching his clothing; he did not first take her out to dinner and then hang out on the couch alone in a dark room with her.

Years ago, President David O. McKay gave an analogy that illustrates the need to escape temptation early. As two men in a rowboat were going down a river, someone from the shore shouted, "The rapids are in front of you and are followed by a waterfall!" The men ignored the warning because, at the time, the boat was easily under control.

Soon the water began increasing in speed. Then, "the men became a little worried and tried to get the boat to shore. But it was too late. The current was too powerful, and over the falls they went to their death. Their fate could have been avoided had they listened to the warning voice."[95]

Indeed, well before the waterfall, escape is easy. When we ride the rapids too close to the edge, however, we may not be able to escape the waterfall's deadly pull.

Like repentance—which, when procrastinated, can become almost impossible—*withstanding temptations can become nearly impossible if we delay our opportunity to escape.* Paul wrote to the Saints in Corinth: "There hath no temptation taken you but such as is common to man: but God is faithful, who will not suffer you to be tempted above that ye are able; but will with the temptation also make a way to escape, that ye may be able to bear it" (1 Corinthians 10:13).

This scripture is usually cited as an encouragement that we will not be tempted more than we are able to overcome. However, Paul doesn't say there are infinite ways to escape from temptation and that we can choose whatever way we see fit. Instead, God makes "*a* way to escape" (emphasis added).[96]

A drug addict, aching for a fix and alone with a bottle of pills, may not be able to withstand that temptation. There was a way for her to escape, but fighting an addiction by herself and with drugs on hand is not that way. A young man in the bedroom of a beautiful girl may find himself in the same situation. Just like it is with the waterfall, the "way to escape" always comes far before the current's draw is too strong. *We can escape all temptations; we cannot necessarily escape them at the last possible minute.*

It takes humility to recognize not only that if you have one drink you will likely have another, but that if you so much as enter the bar you are likely to have that first drink. It takes humility to agree that you are better off not dating until you are sixteen, and even then that you ought to group date first. It takes humility to say that, for you, as a married man or woman, it's best not to take personal lunches alone with a coworker of the opposite sex. It takes humility to bury the sword (as did the Anti-Nephi-Lehies). It takes humility to know that even when our "spirit indeed is willing . . . the flesh is weak" (Matthew 26:41). It takes humility to admit that in certain situations, if we let things go too far, some temptations are simply more than we can bear.

A Disposition to Do No More Evil Is Focused on our Thoughts and Intentions

I used to wonder why, during the Sermon on the Mount, the Savior equated seemingly little acts with the gravest sins. Instead of the commandment, "Thou shalt not kill," he said that just being angry or calling hurtful names caused someone to be "in danger of hell fire" (Matthew 5:21–22). And while "it was said by them of old time, Thou shalt not commit adultery," under the Savior's new direction, "whosoever [merely] looketh on a woman to lust after her hath committed adultery with her already in his heart" (Matthew 5:27–28).

> We can escape all temptations; we cannot necessarily escape them at the last possible minute.

Most of us see a chasm between lust—a sin arguably committed by every man or woman more than we'd like to admit—and adultery. The relative gravity of these different acts seems incomparable. So why did the Savior make the comparison?

I have since found this correlation useful:

Prior to the Savior's ministry, religion predominantly focused on outwardly demonstrated actions: don't murder, don't steal, don't commit adultery. This focus is simple in some ways, but it also can make true obedience more difficult. Perhaps Christ knew that *obedience increases when we focus more on our desires than on the resulting acts.* It's true: spurts of self-control are not as effective or permanent as control over our thoughts and intentions.

As President Kimball put it, "The time to protect against the calamity is when the thought begins to shape itself. Destroy the seed and the plant will never grow."[97] Thought control is fundamental.

We know we shouldn't think about sin, because "as [a man] thinketh in his heart, so is he" (Proverbs 23:7). So, on what should we be focusing? Avoiding sin? Not really.

Our Disposition and Thoughts Should Not Just Focus on Avoiding Temptation

Paul wrote, "Whatsoever things are true, whatsoever things are honest, whatsoever things are just, whatsoever things are pure, whatsoever things are lovely, whatsoever things are of good report; if there be any virtue, and if there be any praise, think on these things" (Philippians 4:8). Note that Paul does not suggest we spend time thinking about avoiding temptation.

Driver's education classes teach students to focus on their own lane and the road ahead. In contrast, drivers who keep watching obstacles they want to avoid—like oncoming traffic in the other lane or trees off the side of the road—are inclined to run straight into them. Driving through life, we should not dwell on what we are trying to avoid; instead, we need to focus on where we want to go.

> Obedience increases when we focus more on our desires than on the resulting acts.

Christ demonstrated this principle when He taught a law higher than the Ten Commandments. Rather than a list of "thou shalt nots," He gave us the Beatitudes. Instead of focusing on a list of ten things not to do, He explained that all commandments fit under two positive directions: love God and love your neighbor. Loving God and loving your neighbor are pure, honest, just, lovely, virtuous, and praiseworthy things. In fact, the very definition of sin focuses on the positive: "to him that knoweth to do good, and doeth it not, to him it is sin" (James 4:17).

A positive focus is also more effective from a neurological perspective. It's difficult for our minds to negate images and thoughts. Try this: don't think of a rhinoceros. Did you think of a rhinoceros? I bet you did. Before we can avoid a specific thought, our brains first have to conjure up the unwanted thing. So, despite our best intentions, not every part of our mind or nervous system cooperates. Certain brain mechanisms, when activated, respond to unwanted thoughts or images as just another goal, and biological autopilot programs are aroused immediately, regardless of our intentions.[98] Thus, *even a temporary negative focus on temptation can prolong our inclination toward it.*

> Even a temporary negative focus on temptation can prolong our inclination toward it.

Bruce Fordham of LDS Family Services gave similar counsel in the *Ensign*: "Think about how *you* respond to a negative or inappropriate thought that comes into your mind, either as a result of unhealthy thought patterns or simply because you are a natural man or woman (see Mosiah 3:19; D&C 67:12). Perhaps you reprimand yourself. Or maybe you repeatedly tell yourself to stop thinking about that subject. In the case of the first response, you unwittingly weaken your resistance to such thoughts and lower your sense of self-worth and confidence. With the second response, you unknowingly give energy and strength to the undesirable thought by repeating its image. This occurs because our brains are unable to replace something with nothing. When there is not another thought or activity to replace a negative one, the thought to open the cupboard or miss the field goal or eat the cake takes root because of the image's repetition in the vulnerable mind."[99]

Moreover, given our innate drive to maintain and exercise our God-given (and fought-for[100]) agency, the more frequently we tell ourselves "you can't do X" or "you shouldn't do Y," the more subconsciously inclined we may be to rebel. After all, this entire earth life is about exercising our agency. In the words of President David O. McKay, "Next to the bestowal of life itself, the right to direct that life is God's greatest gift to man."[101] We need to know we are making positive choices to direct our life, not just rebelling or fighting against negative ones. This is essential in order for us to clarify our true desires.

These principles also help maintain a more effective focus on the commandments. You can't fully obey the Word of Wisdom, for example, if you are only thinking about it as a Pharisaical list of prohibitions. Let's be honest: do you seriously think it's wise to chug a whole liter of full-sugar Pepsi or to drink two energy drinks every morning when you shouldn't have one glass of green tea? Does that seem right to you? Are you honestly obeying the spirit of the Word of Wisdom if you overeat fast food every day? This isn't to say that anyone can "perfectly obey" the spirit of the Word of Wisdom. Still, instead of thinking only "I can't drink, smoke, or do drugs," we are less "slothful" and far more "wise" when we focus on strengthening our desire to keep our body in top condition (D&C 58:26).

Similarly, instead of seeing the law of chastity as a rule to not do anything sexual with people you aren't married to, we could focus on the positive: "love thy [husband or] wife with all thy heart, and cleave unto [him or] her and none else" (D&C 42:22).

There are infinite ways every one of us could better demonstrate our love and become a better spouse.

When my daughter Ella was five, she overheard me grumbling about not finding our bottle of wrinkle releaser. I was late for an event and had a shirt with wrinkles in it. Eager to help, Ella got excited.

"Dad, I know where the wrinkle releaser is!" she exclaimed.

"You do?"

"Yeah, come on. I'll show you."

I was thrilled. The day was saved. Ella took my hand and led me into the laundry room. "Here it is, Dad," she said, pointing to the iron and ironing board. "Do you want me to show you how to use it?"

If I had been helping out more around the house, perhaps my five-year-old wouldn't think she needed to show me how an iron works. Admittedly, although I did know how it worked, I never used it. Helping out around the house without being asked is one of the countless ways we can demonstrate love. And focusing on love as opposed to avoiding temptation is far more effective in keeping us on the Lord's perfect path.

Focusing on Christ Is the Best Way to Overcome Temptation

When Peter sank after walking on water, Christ asked, "Wherefore didst thou doubt?" (Matthew 14:31). The moment Peter took his focus off the Savior—exactly like that inexperienced driver watching an obstacle off the road—he lost the power to stand up, let alone to keep moving. To maintain a change of heart, we should not focus on temptations we are trying to avoid, but instead focus "wholly upon the merits of him who is mighty to save" (2 Nephi 31:19). The hymn sums it up perfectly: "Temptations lose their pow'r when thou art nigh."[102] When Christ is near to our hearts and minds, temptations have no hold over us.

The scriptures constantly emphasize that when we *rely* upon our own strength, we will be *left* to our own strength (see Helaman 4:13; see also Mormon 2:26). We don't want this. The arm of flesh is weak.

Alma's description of experiencing a mighty change of heart is the largest chiasmus in the Book of Mormon, lasting the entire thirty-sixth chapter of Alma. (Chiasmus is a structure that uses parallel clauses to focus on a central theme or point, often found in Hebrew poetry.) In Alma's lengthy chiasmus, his primary focus becomes incredibly clear: "I remembered . . . Jesus Christ, a Son of God, . . . [and] I cried within my heart: O Jesus, thou Son of God, have mercy on me" (Alma 36:17–18).[103]

> We are not simply to become less like Satan. We are to become more like Christ.

Thus, the largest piece of chiasmus in the Book of Mormon emphasizes one thing: receiving a mighty change of heart and avoiding sin requires focusing on the Savior. The crux of Alma's mighty change is a focus on Jesus Christ as the Son of God.

Following his conversion, Alma counseled the Saints to "teach them to withstand every temptation of the devil with their faith on the Lord Jesus Christ" (Alma 37:33). He could have filled a book with techniques on how to withstand temptation by increased discipline and motivational techniques. Instead, he prescribed this single method: faith in Jesus Christ.

Ultimately, the secret to overcoming temptation is not about willpower exercises, therapy, or snapping a rubber band on your wrist whenever you slip. *We are not simply to become less like Satan. We are to become more like Christ.* Thus, the most effective focus is not avoiding temptation; it is the Savior.[104]

This solution can be deceptively simple. Alma gave the following parting advice to his son Helaman: "O my son, do not let us be slothful because of the easiness of the way; for so was it with our fathers; for so was it prepared for them, that if they would look they might live; even so it is with us. The way is prepared, and if we will look we may live forever. And now, my son, see that ye take care of these sacred things, yea, see that ye look to God and live" (Alma 37:46–47).

Here, Alma referenced the Old Testament account in which the Israelites were suffering the effects of being bitten by poisonous serpents. Instead of various complicated methods to remove poison or prepare antidotes, the Lord commanded His people, through the prophet Moses, to look to a brazen serpent on a staff, representative of the Savior. It was then, and it is today, that simple.

Stop thinking about temptations you are trying to avoid. Stop looking at your habitual sins "off the side of the road." Stop fearing and doubting your ability to overcome the devil's flaxen cords. Instead, "Look unto [God] in every thought; doubt not, fear not" (D&C 6:36). Fill your days with thoughts and teachings of the Savior. "Look to God and live."

KEY POINTS

MAINTAINING THE MIGHTY CHANGE BY A CHARACTER NOT DISPOSED TO DO EVIL

Qualities of a character that is not disposed to do evil:

1. Avoids proximity to enticing sins.

2. Escapes temptation at an early stage, while still able.

3. Focuses on thoughts and intentions, not just actions.

4. Ultimately—and most importantly—focuses on Christ, not just avoiding sin.

CHAPTER 8

A DISPOSITION TO DO GOOD CONTINUALLY

Wherefore, I, Moroni, am commanded to write these things that evil may be done away, and that the time may come that Satan may have no power upon the hearts of the children of men, but that they may be persuaded to do good continually, that they may come unto the fountain of all righteousness and be saved.

ETHER 8:26

King Benjamin explained that in addition to losing our appetite for sin, those who have mighty changes of heart also "do good continually" (Mosiah 5:2). There are two noteworthy components here: (1) we need to remain disposed to doing good, and (2) we need to do so continually.

Focus on Doing Good

After experiencing a mighty change of heart, the Apostle Paul changed his name from Saul and declared his new focus. "Abhor that which is evil," he told the Romans, and "cleave to that which is good" (Romans 12:9). He then advised: "Be not overcome of evil, but *overcome evil with good*" (v. 21; emphasis added).

Every good habit we bring into our lives adds another fortification against the devil's influence. In Matthew, the Savior provides an allegory: "When the unclean spirit is gone out of a man, he walketh through dry places, seeking rest, and findeth none. Then he saith, I will return into my house from whence I came out; and when he is come, he findeth it empty, swept, and garnished. Then goeth he, and taketh with himself seven other spirits more wicked than himself, and they enter in and dwell there: and the last state of that man is worse than the first" (Matthew 12:43–45).

Like the man who became free from an unclean spirit but failed to replace it with good, *when we experience a change of heart we must fill our lives with good or Satan may intrude once again, perhaps even more completely.*

Because "good" itself is the preeminent weapon to overcome evil, good actions and thoughts should receive our continuous attention and effort. Thankfully, there are infinite ways we can build "good" fortifications against the enemy before an attack occurs (like Captain Moroni in Alma 50:1–6, 10) without focusing on fear, doubt, or other negative emotions.

Good activities range from the overtly spiritual, such as prayer, scripture study, and temple attendance, to things like spending time with our families and working on physical development.

> When we experience a change of heart we must replace past sins with new good behavior, or Satan may intrude once again.

Hearing/Reading the Word of God

As one of my former missionary companions came out of the waters of baptism with a former investigator, a homemade black chest tattoo shone through the elder's clinging, wet shirt. His ears were scarred from multiple earrings he had worn in the past. Obvious to all, this elder had once experienced a serious change. Ironically, that conversion had been instigated years before by a Jehovah's Witness.

Well before he was a missionary, this elder was a teenager in northern Utah who spent his time hanging out with homeless kids, dumpster diving, stealing pizza, taking drugs, and experimenting with the occult. We'll call him David. One day when he was high and alone in a small house in Brigham City, a Jehovah's Witness and his young son knocked on the door. Bored, David let them come inside and listened to their message.

David had grown up in the LDS Church, but at that point he didn't think he had a testimony anymore, if he'd ever had one at all. But he was curious about the message shared by these Jehovah's Witnesses. So they came again. On the next visit, the father and son read scriptures with David, and something stirred within him. He disagreed with them. He interpreted verses differently than they did. He suddenly realized that—after all these years and lifestyle changes—he still had a testimony of at least some LDS doctrine. "What do I really believe?" he asked himself. He decided to find out.

David started reading the scriptures again. And the Spirit bore witness. David prayed, went to church, and met the bishop. He told the bishop that he wanted to change his life, asked how to do it, and *did it.* He took out his earrings, threw away a full carton of cigarettes, flushed his marijuana and other drugs down the toilet, repented, and prepared to serve a mission. After General Authority consent—with David innocently showing up at the Church Office Building interview in jeans and a T-shirt—he was sent on a mission to South Carolina. We experienced more success together than I had with any other companion during two years of missionary service.

Like the experience of my former companion, the accounts of Alma and King Benjamin also demonstrate how scripture provokes a mighty change of heart. Alma the Younger reminded the

Saints of Zarahemla that the Lord "delivered [their forefathers'] souls from hell" and "changed their hearts . . . by the light of the everlasting word" (Alma 5:6–7).

This change began, Alma explained, when his own father (Alma the Elder) had "a mighty change wrought in his heart" after hearing scripture preached by the prophet Abinadi (Alma 5:11–12). Thereafter, Alma the Elder "preached the word unto [their] fathers, and a mighty change was also wrought in their hearts" as well (v. 13).

It was also preaching the word of God that "wrought a mighty change in [the people of King Benjamin], or in [their] hearts" (Mosiah 4:1–3; 5:1–2). Like my mission companion and Christians of two thousand years ago, we too can receive (and

> The word of God has a greater tendency to lead people to do good than anything else.

maintain) a mighty change of heart as a result of hearing and reading the word of God.

We know that *the word of God has a greater tendency to lead people to do good than anything else.* To prevent a conspiracy between the Zoramites and Lamanites, instead of going to battle, Alma took Ammon, Aaron, Omner, Amulek, Zeezrom, and two of his sons to preach to the Zoramites (see Alma 31:1–7). He wrote: "And now, as the preaching of the word had a great tendency to lead the people to do that which was just—yea, it had had more powerful effect upon the minds of the people than the sword, or anything else, which had happened unto them— therefore Alma thought it was expedient that they should try the virtue of the word of God" (v. 5).

The Book of Mormon is particularly effective in changing lives. President Benson testified that it imparts "greater power to resist temptation. You will find the power to avoid deception. You will find the power to stay on the strait and narrow path. The scriptures are called 'the words of life' (D&C 84:85), and nowhere is that more true than it is of the Book of Mormon."[105]

I have found that when you are searching the scriptures with a specific purpose in mind—to understand some concept better or to find answers to questions you are struggling with—scripture study becomes so much more powerful and exciting. Reading without any questions in mind or topics you want to explore is like not asking God any questions in prayer—He doesn't have a chance to provide you with answers. As the Savior proclaimed, "he that hath the scriptures, let him search them" (3 Nephi 10:14). Going beyond "reading" the scriptures to actually "searching" them gives your study focus. Undoubtedly, when you truly search the scriptures, rather than just passively reading for whatever pops out, you will find yourself "ponder[ing] continually upon the things" you've read—while you are in the shower, lying in bed, or driving in the car (2 Nephi 4:16.). You will write down inspiration that comes to you throughout the day. Like an explorer eager for a new discovery, you will look forward to the next round of scripture study to continue on your search.

Searching scripture also helps correct the earthly wisdom we inevitably encounter. Remember, "even the humble followers of Christ . . . are misled, that in *many instances* they do *err* because they are taught by the precepts of men" (2 Nephi 28:14; emphasis added). Worldly knowledge is polluted with the precepts of men and, as Joseph Smith explained, "one truth revealed from heaven is worth all the sectarian notions in existence."[106]

From what constitutes a planet to whether certain foods are good or bad for you, science is always changing. Scriptural truth revealed from heaven, however, never does.

Hugh Nibley said it best: "Science, philosophy, and common sense all have a right to their day in court. But the last word does not lie with them. Every time men in their wisdom have come forth with the last word, other words have promptly followed. The last word is a testimony of the gospel that comes only by direct revelation. Our Father in heaven speaks it, and if it were in perfect agreement with the science of today, it would surely be out of line with the science of tomorrow. Let us not, therefore, seek to hold God to the learned opinions of the moment when He speaks the language of eternity."[107]

For all of these reasons, hearing and reading the word of God is a particularly effective means of overcoming evil with good and maintaining a mighty change of heart.

Mental/Educational Development

Cram your heads full of knowledge.
—PRESIDENT GORDON B. HINCKLEY[108]

We can do good by focusing on educational development. "Shall I sit down and read the Bible, the Book of Mormon, and the Book of Covenants all the time?" asked Brigham Young. "Yes, if you please, and when you have done, you may be nothing more than a sectarian after all. It is your duty to study . . . everything upon the face of the earth, in addition to reading those books."[109]

On another occasion, he admonished the Saints: "Learn everything that the children of men know. Every true principle, every true science, every art and the knowledge that men possess, or that they ever did or ever will possess, is from God."[110] "We are trying to teach this people to use their brains."[111]

Why is it so important that we "use [our] brains"? Brigham Young explained: "All our educational pursuits are . . . that we may become fit subjects to dwell in a higher state of existence and intelligence than we now enjoy" and "[i]f men would be great in goodness, they must be intelligent."[112] In fact, *the very "glory of God," Himself, is "intelligence"* (D&C 93:26).

President Gordon B. Hinckley gave excellent counsel in this area: "Be smart. The Lord wants you to educate your minds and hands, whatever your chosen field. Whether it be repairing refrigerators, or the work of a skilled surgeon, you must train yourselves. Seek for the best schooling available. Become a workman of integrity in the world that lies ahead of you. I repeat, you will bring honor to the Church and you will be generously blessed because of that training. There can be no doubt, none whatever, that education pays. Do not short-circuit your lives. If you do so, you will pay for it over and over and over again."[113]

Physical Development—Exercise and Diet

We can also do good by focusing on physical goals. Care for our body is important for many reasons. The Holy Spirit—a member of the Godhead—literally dwells within us (see 1 Corinthians 6:19). To feel His presence continually, we must maintain a suitable vessel.

Conversely, Satan's attitude toward physical bodies also reveals their significance. Mutilations and sacrifices that disrespect and harm the flesh (of man as well as animals) are fundamental practices among so-called "devil worshippers." Because Satan never received the blessing of a body (see Revelation 12:9), he wants us to disrespect God by mistreating our bodies in every way possible.

Caring for our physical welfare also brings a happier, more balanced life. Physical health allows for increased mental clarity and emotional balance and demonstrates our spiritual priorities. Like fasting, exercise can bring us closer to the Lord as we subjugate the flesh's lazy tendencies for a higher purpose.

As Latter-day Saints, we have a divine charge in this area. Unfortunately, some of us take the letter of the law seriously but completely forget the spirit of it. Caught up in numerous prohibitions, we miss the forest for the trees.

With the Word of Wisdom, for example, instead of being known for lists of prohibitions (which could never encompass all the things we should or should not partake of[114]), Latter-day Saints ought to be recognized as the most healthy people in the world. We should be known for our attention and adherence to revelation and modern science regarding every aspect of healthy living.

As proclaimed in a recent general conference, "Please use good judgment in what and especially how much you eat, and regularly give your body the exercise it needs and deserves. If you are physically able, decide today to be the master of your own house and begin a regular, long-term exercise program, suited to your abilities, combined with a healthier diet."[115] Study the best ways to care for your body and act accordingly. After a mighty change of heart, this is an excellent way to keep idle hands busy and to "overcome evil with good" (Romans 12:21).

In short, even seemingly "nonspiritual" activities such as physical and educational development are inspired means of "doing good continually" that those who have experienced a mighty change will find great value in pursuing.

Social Development—Time with Family and Friends or Missionary Work

Max: *Mom, Jesus would like it if every day was Sunday, wouldn't He?*

Mom: *Yeah, probably.*

Max: *But that would drive people crazy . . . and wear out their Sunday clothes.*

Max wears out his Sunday clothes regardless of how many days a week he wears them. But he does have a point. Even the Lord gave us only one Sabbath out of seven days. Moreover, "doing good continuously" can also be accomplished by social development and healthy interaction with family and friends all days of the week.

Elder Rex D. Pinegar related the following: "Charles Francis Adams, the grandson of the second president of the United States, was a successful lawyer, a member of the U.S. House of Representatives, and U.S. ambassador to Britain. Amidst his responsibilities, he had little time to spare. He did, however, keep a diary. One day he wrote, 'Went fishing with my son today—a day wasted!'

"On that same date, Charles's son, Brooks Adams, had printed in his own diary, 'Went fishing with my father today—the most wonderful day of my life.'"[116]

No matter how much time and effort we spend, we can all be better sons, daughters, brothers, sisters, fathers, and mothers. In fact, the family unit provides some of the most powerful opportunities to experience charity, the pure love of Christ. As with every other circumstance in life, the Lord placed us in certain families for a reason. Giving life, food, or counsel to a family member can be among our most meaningful experiences.

Not only are we doing good, lessons learned within our families are essential educational opportunities. Learning to become a better father, mother, husband, or wife is surely at least as important as learning to become a better electrician or accountant. Elder Neal A. Maxwell explained, "Sometimes we make so many commitments that they become like the vines in the allegory of Jacob, threatening to 'overcome the roots,' including the 'roots' of family relationships."[117] On a different occasion, he asked, "Given the gravity of current conditions, would parents be willing to give up just one outside thing, giving that time and talent instead to the family?"[118]

We also bless the lives of our spiritual families—the world is full of our brothers and sisters—by strengthening those relationships. It's unfortunate how often we talk about increasing member missionary work without mentioning the need to have more friends of other faiths. As the saying goes, "People don't care how much you know until they know how much you care." Inviting people to meet with the missionaries or attend church is fantastic. Without first building a foundation of real compassion and friendship, though, many of us risk coming across like security system or pest control salesmen.

Missionary work often feels uncomfortable for members because it *is* uncomfortable. But it doesn't have to be—and probably shouldn't be. We may feel fake because we are being fake—doing what we think we *should* do instead of what we sincerely *want* to do. In contrast, when you become actual friends with nonmembers, when you *really do* care about their lives and they *know you care,* talking about whether they are happy with their church or want to check out your church are natural, comfortable questions. *We will undoubtedly experience more blessings from missionary work when we develop more and better relationships with persons of other faiths.*

> We will undoubtedly experience more blessings from missionary work when we develop more and better relationships with persons of other faiths.

Lastly, members need help, too. Perfecting the Saints is just as important as proclaiming the gospel. We are not just members of a religion; we are members of a Church. Our organization is full of imperfect people (including an imperfect, unpaid clergy) all charged with building each other up. All of these relationships are ways of "doing good" that bless our lives and maintain the mighty change of heart.

We Should Focus on Doing Good *Continually*

Maintaining a disposition to do good requires continuous dedication. Moroni explained that everything which "is of God inviteth and enticeth to do good *continually*" (Moroni 7:13; emphasis added). Speaking to his son Corianton, Alma counseled him to "do good *continually*" (Alma 41:14; emphasis added).

Ether describes those who "[believe] in God" as "*always* abounding in good works" (Ether 12:4; emphasis added). Alma counseled his son Helaman to teach people "to *never be weary* of good works" (Alma 37:34; emphasis added). In the great sermon on the seed of faith (which becomes the tree of life), Alma advised that failure to nourish the tree with "great diligence" would cause it to wither away (Alma 32:38–43).

We must be continuous in our efforts to do good because we are so quick to forget. Our attention span for righteousness and the speed at which Satan can rebind his flaxen cords is astounding. As Mormon lamented, "Thus we see how quick the children of men do forget the Lord their God, yea, how quick to do iniquity, and to be led away by the evil one" (Alma 46:8).

This sad fate befell the Jaredites, who, despite having experienced "miracles" and "marvelous works," were "slothful, and forgot to exercise their faith and diligence and then those marvelous works ceased, and they did not progress in their journey" (Alma 37:41). We must not overestimate our ability to fight temptation without exercising continual and diligent efforts for good.

Thankfully, scriptures emphasize good activities we should

continually pursue. Three of the most repeated invitations in the scriptures are calls for continuous prayer, repentance, and remembering the miracles we have witnessed.

Pray Continually

Twenty years ago, a strung-out teenager came to my parents' house and asked to clean their windows with newspaper. Addicted to drugs and living on the street, he would occasionally take a bus to their neighborhood, do odd jobs around the house, and stay for dinner. Late one night, he showed up with bruises on his face and tears streaming down his cheeks. He had been beaten up. He didn't want any money; he just said he was leaving town and going home.

When he got home, his mother brought him to a church meeting in which the congregation was asked to give up their sins and ask Christ to heal them. This teenager stood, and in response to humble prayer, he felt a change that he describes as running from the top of his head to the soles of his feet.

> We must be continuous in our efforts to do good because we are so quick to forget.

Years later, this man showed up at my parents' doorstep—drug free, with a wife, a new suit, and a new car. He had become a preacher and started his own successful business to help get people off drugs and off the street. My father attributes his ability to maintain this change—initiated by prayer—to being a man who prays more frequently than anyone he has ever known.

Continual prayer is an attribute of those who received a mighty change of heart and continue to "feel so now" (Alma 5:26). King Benjamin promised that those who experienced a mighty change of heart will "*always* rejoice, and be filled with the love of God, and *always* retain a remission of your sins" if they are "*calling on the name of the Lord daily,* and standing steadfastly in the faith of that which is to come" (Mosiah 4:11–12; emphasis added). Amulek counseled, "When you do not cry unto the Lord, let your hearts be full, drawn out in *prayer unto him continually* for your welfare, and also for the welfare of those who are around you" (Alma 34:27; emphasis added).

Praying continually also brings blessings including prosperity and strength to overcome temptation. After the Nephites received a mighty change of heart and repented, they "did pray unto the Lord their God *continually,* insomuch that the Lord did bless them, according to his word, so that they did wax strong and prosper in the land" (Alma 62:51; emphasis added).

As mentioned earlier, Alma counseled that we "watch and pray *continually,* that [we] may not be tempted above that which [we] can bear" (Alma 13:28; emphasis added). Amulek similarly exhorted that we "be watchful unto prayer *continually,* that [we] may not be led away by the temptations of the devil, *that he may not overpower [us],* that [we] may not become his subjects at the last day" (Alma 34:39; emphasis added).[119]

At times, our repetitive sins feel "above [what we] can bear." They probably are. We must stop relying on our own arms of flesh and start "finding strength beyond [our] own."[120] And that miraculous strength comes from continual prayer.

Repent Continually (and Immediately)

Who is righteous? Anyone who is repenting. No matter how bad he has been, if he is repenting he is a righteous man. There is hope for him. And no matter how good he has been all his life, if he is not repenting, he is a wicked man. The difference is which way you are facing. The man on the top of the stairs facing down is much worse off than the man on the bottom step who is facing up. The direction we are facing, that is repentance; and that is what determines whether we are good or bad.

—HUGH NIBLEY[121]

At dinner one night, my son Jackson took the Lord's name in vain. I suspect he hears the phrase nonstop in school, but that was the first time I'd heard him use it. After I explained why it was inappropriate, he apologized. I then asked Jackson to say the blessing on the food.

"Dear Heavenly Father," he began, "Thank you for everything you've given me. Sorry I called you 'God' today. . . ."

Although perhaps Jackson didn't fully understand what he did wrong by calling Heavenly Father "God," he did know to repent immediately. That's exactly what we need to do.

Receiving a mighty change does not eliminate the need to keep repenting. For example, after changing from a "sinful man" (Luke 5:8) to an Apostle who witnessed countless miracles, walked on water, and witnessed the visitation of glorified beings on the Mount of Transfiguration, even Peter still had mortal failings. In the Garden of Gethsemane, Peter fell asleep instead of keeping watch, and he denied knowing the Savior on three occasions (see Matthew 26:69–74).

Remember, we each have a conversion *story*, not a conversion sentence. We will all sin again. Therefore, to retain that mighty change, we must "apply the principle of repentance continually."[122]

Elder J. Golden Kimball allegedly said he wouldn't be judged in the hereafter for using colorful language because, as he put it, "I repent too damn fast."[123] In a recent general conference, Elder Jörg Klebingat said we should "become really, really good at repenting thoroughly and quickly."[124]

Brigham Young also advocated the "secret" of immediate

repentance: "I do not recollect that I have seen five minutes since I was baptized that I have not been ready to preach a funeral sermon, lay hands on the sick, or to pray in private or in public. *I will tell you the secret of this.* In all your business transactions, words, and communications, if you commit an overt act, *repent of that immediately,* and call upon God to deliver you from evil and give you the light of His spirit."[125]

Perhaps there is nothing so fantastic as the Lord's promise, "Yea, and as often as my people repent will I forgive them their trespasses against me" (Mosiah 26:30).

Immediate repentance is a "secret," as Brigham Young put it, for multiple reasons. First, as Elder Talmage taught (and as discussed in chapter 1), procrastinating repentance can result in an inability to repent.[126] Just like the Nephites whose experience with this led to their destruction, delayed repentance hardens hearts and returns us to the cycle of pride, making it very difficult to repent.

Be Careful with Guilt

Second, we should not live for any extended period of time with guilt, because the "fruits of the Spirit" (e.g., love, joy, peace, and so on) are incompatible with guilt. This doesn't mean that we should never feel guilt. Guilt is a sign that our heart is not yet too hard. However, guilt—when it is true godly sorrow[127]—is only useful insofar as it motivates decisive repentance.

Alma explained this to his son Corianton: "And now, my son, I desire that ye should let these things trouble you no more, and *only* let your sins trouble you, with that trouble which shall bring you down unto repentance" (Alma 42:29; emphasis added). Guilt should last to the extent that it is needed to motivate permanent change and should thereafter be replaced by "love, joy, peace," and other fruits of the Spirit (Galatians 5:22).

Guilt can lead to terrible consequences when it is not used for repentance and subsequently replaced by God's love. Look at the examples of Peter and Judas. To one degree or another, both men failed in their apostolic charges to be special witnesses for Jesus Christ.[128] Peter "denied [Christ] with an oath," saying "I do not know the man" (Matthew 26:72). Ironically, Judas sinned by doing the opposite—identifying Christ to one of the chief priests (see Matthew 26:14–16; 47–50). Realizing what he'd done, Peter "wept bitterly" (v. 75). Judas also was overcome with remorse and cast the thirty pieces of silver he had received into the temple. Instead of experiencing a change of heart like Peter, however, guilt consumed Judas. He "went and hanged himself" (Matthew 27:5).

When not followed by repentance and the Spirit's peace, guilt can be overwhelming and lead to depression. In the song "Shots," by Imagine Dragons,[129] I know my brother Dan was expressing those destructive emotions when he wrote these lyrics:

Oh, I'm going to mess this up
Oh, this is just my luck
Over and over and over again
I'm sorry for everything
Oh, everything I've done
From the second that I was born it seems I had a loaded gun
And then I shot, shot, shot a hole through everything I loved
Oh, I shot, shot, shot a hole through every single thing that I loved

None of us should live for any time—even "five minutes," as Brigham Young suggested—without the presence of the Holy Ghost. Elder F. Enzio Busche declared that "we, as members of the Church, should not be satisfied to be one single moment of our waking hours without the insightful, powerful influence of the Spirit."[130] We don't just need Him every day; we "need [Him] every hour."[131]

Perhaps this is why the sacrament is such a frequent (and essential) ordinance. We need the sacrament weekly because we cannot afford to have the emotional and spiritual baggage of any more time building up. We must be cleansed. As Elder M. Russell Ballard explained, "Transgression of any kind is always accompanied by a loss of self-esteem."[132] That loss inevitably leads to further transgressions. And our loving Father does not want us to carry this yoke alone. Purposeful use of the sacrament allows us to start each new week like newly baptized children.

Our weekly services are also a time to help each other feel *only* the kind of guilt that leads to repentance. As fellow brothers and sisters, we should be sensitive in how we interact with each other, motivating repentance without encouraging someone to be consumed by guilt and shame. Too many of us—even when clothed in white shirts and ties—feel uniquely weak, uniquely shameful, and uniquely alone. Instead of exacerbating depression, we should choose our words and deeds carefully to help one another feel the unconditional love of God.

In short, the consequences of unrepented sin are unbearable. Our hearts harden, the Spirit withdraws, and the resultant spiritual and emotional baggage causes damage we cannot afford. There is no shame in sincere repentance, regardless of how frequently it occurs.

Continually Remember the Miracles in Your Life

Like continual prayer and repentance, always remembering life's miracles helps us maintain a mighty change of heart. King Benjamin promised that we will "always rejoice, and be filled with the love of God, and always retain a remission of your sins" if we "*always retain in remembrance,* the greatness of God, and [our] own nothingness, and his goodness and long-suffering towards [us], unworthy creatures, and humble [our]selves even in the depths of humility" (Mosiah 4:11–12; emphasis added).

After experiencing mighty changes of heart, Amulek taught the Zoramites to "*live in thanksgiving daily,* for the many mercies and blessings which [the Lord] doth bestow upon you" (Alma 34:38; emphasis added).

Similarly, Alma asked new converts, "Have you *sufficiently retained in remembrance* the captivity of your fathers? Yea, and have you *sufficiently retained in remembrance* his mercy and long-suffering towards them? And moreover, have ye *sufficiently retained in remembrance* that he has delivered their souls from hell?" (Alma 5:6; emphasis added). He wanted them to remember the miracles the Lord had granted "sufficiently," and sufficient remembrance requires continuousness. The prophet Nephi recognized this when he stated that his "heart pondereth *continually* upon the things which [he had] seen and heard" (2 Nephi 4:16; emphasis added).

We need to continually remember the countless ways the Lord blesses us because, again, we are so prone to forget. Within twenty years of Christ's visit to the Nephites, the son of Helaman described a sad pattern of the Nephite people. It took only one year to change from a righteous people who remembered their God to a people who forgot him and began to "wax strong in iniquity" (Helaman 11:34–36).

There was a time when the Nephites were both prosperous and (simultaneously) humble. How was it possible to maintain that delicate balance? The key was a continual remembrance of the "great things the Lord had done for them" (Alma 62:50).

Our lives overflow with acts of divine intervention. These miracles range from an inspired mission call to getting into that

perfect school to the improbable birth of healthy children to finding a fulfilling job to falling in love and getting married. We have
all had prayers answered that surpass random probability, and we
cannot afford to forget them.

On a personal note, managing a successful rock band (let
alone an LDS-fronted one) is something I never expected to do.
This combination of using my law degree with creative and business abilities was not on my radar. I could never have orchestrated this or obtained that job on my own. I have no doubt that
Heavenly Father planned this, and I am grateful to have been
given the opportunity.

The statistics were even more stacked against my younger
brother Dan's career. As the seventh son, Dan's older brothers include three lawyers (two of whom are also managers), a dentist, a
plastic surgeon, and an anesthesiologist. Unlike his older siblings,
Dan decided to drop out of college to try to make a career singing
in a rock band.

You can imagine my parents' concern. I will never forget the
anxious conversations in which my mom asked me what Dan's
chances were of his band "making it." After all, she expressed,
it had happened for the Killers, right? I told her the statistical
chances were zero. Endless passionate, talented musicians try and
fail at making careers in the music business every day.

Yet despite seemingly impossible odds, my brother's band,
Imagine Dragons, has sold millions of albums and is touring
the world. Within a few short years, they won a Grammy, set
a Billboard record for having a song on the top-40 chart longer
than any song in history, and one year sold more albums than any
other rock band that year.

Did Dan deserve this success? No way. Sure, he worked hard
with the talent God had blessed him with. But he certainly didn't

deserve anything. This is a miracle, like many other aspects of our lives, and no one is entitled to a miracle. Just like He did with Gideon's army, our Heavenly Father is so benevolent that He occasionally grants miracles that are statistically impossible to help us to recognize their source.

Still, too often we either forget these great blessings or think we accomplished them on our own! Perhaps we are fast to forget because we aren't used to receiving significant gifts we didn't earn (particularly a problem for those obsessed with "fairness"). For example, fifteen years ago, my brother Dan destroyed a gift he'd received because he thought he didn't deserve it.

Growing up, each year our family had an Easter-egg-decorating competition. All of the cousins decorated eggs, and my grandparents gave out cash prizes. One year, my wife decorated an egg that she thought wasn't competition-worthy. So she didn't enter it. But my brother Dan, who was eight years old at the time, disagreed. He liked her egg and put it in the area for judging. As it turns out, Dan was right; her egg won a prize of six dollars. Pleasantly surprised, my wife split the prize money with Dan.

Hours later, my grandfather found three one-dollar bills torn up in a bathroom trashcan. He had lived through the Great Depression and was livid with this waste of money. When Dan admitted to tearing up those dollar bills, my grandfather lit into him. Even though three dollars was also a lot of money to an eight-year-old, Dan didn't want it. Crying, he said he tore those bills up because every time he looked at them, he felt bad. He felt like he didn't deserve the money.

On one level, that intention seems admirable. Dan wanted what he deserved—nothing more and nothing less. But the money was a gift. Whether it was "deserved" is irrelevant. As King Benjamin explained, "Are we not all beggars?" (Mosiah 4:19).

None of us deserves physical salvation—immortality—but we will receive it nonetheless. Nor does any of us deserve spiritual salvation. These gifts are given to those who humbly seek, recognize, and appreciate them. But nobody deserves them. It is the devil who tells us we should get what we deserve, because on our own, all of us deserve nothing but death and hell.

We all want life to be fair, but it isn't, and it wasn't meant to be.

We have also all received miracles of protection—physical and spiritual. The mere fact that we are alive today is a miracle. We don't deserve life or health any more than the billions who have suffered and died before us or the hundreds of thousands who die every single day.

Certainly, each of us can remember times when a wrong turn could have destroyed us. Nephi recognized this when he "groane[d] because of [his] sins" but knew that God had supported and "led [him] through [his] afflictions in the wilderness; and he hath preserved [him] upon the waters of the great deep" (2 Nephi 4:17–20).

It is worth repeating King Benjamin's promise that those who always remember God's miracles in their lives will "always rejoice" (Mosiah 4:12). This is a promise too often overlooked. Instead of finding joy in remembering miracles, the natural man has a plethora of unfulfilling substitutes. For example, although wealth can make life easier, it does not make you "always rejoice." Being famous does not guarantee permanent happiness, either. I've met countless famous people who, if anything, seem more frequently unhappy than non-famous people. Being healthy doesn't guarantee

> If we always remember the countless blessings our Heavenly Father gives—which none of us deserve—the Lord promises us that we will *always rejoice.*

nonstop rejoicing, either. Having wonderful children and a beautiful wife or handsome husband doesn't necessarily mean you are happy or you will "always rejoice." *But if we always remember the countless blessings our Heavenly Father gives—which none of us deserve—the Lord promises us that we will always rejoice.* Grateful people are happy people.

As simple as this sounds, documenting the miracles in your life and continually remembering them is a great secret in maintaining a mighty change of heart and continuing to "feel so now" (Alma 5:26). Perhaps this practice is effective because it helps us remain humble, that great condition to receiving and retaining the mighty change of heart.

"Are you ever burdened with a load of care? / Does the cross seem heavy you are called to bear? / Count your many blessings; ev'ry doubt will fly, / And you will be singing as the days go by."[133]

KEY POINTS

MAINTAINING A MIGHTY CHANGE OF HEART BY A DISPOSITION TO DO GOOD CONTINUALLY

Qualities of a disposition to do good continually:

1. Focuses on affirmatively doing good, not just avoiding sin, through activities such as spiritual development, mental and educational development, physical development, and social development.

2. Focuses on doing good continually by praying continually, repenting continually (and immediately), and continually remembering the miracles in your life.

CHAPTER 9

THE FRUITS OF
A MIGHTY CHANGE

I am as light as a feather, I am as happy as an angel, I am
as merry as a school-boy. I am as giddy as a drunken man.
A merry Christmas to every-body! A happy New Year to
all the world! Hallo here! Whoop! Hallo!

EBENEZER SCROOGE[134]

It is hard to imagine a miracle more joyful than a mighty change
of heart. Alma described this as feeling to "sing the song of redeeming love" (Alma 5:26). Knowing the Lord is on your side
and that, as a result, you can accomplish every righteous desire is
like optimism on steroids.

I can personally recognize the times in my life when I have
felt closest to the will of the Lord. In those times, I feel intense
joy and peace. I feel increased sensitivity to the Spirit and greater
strength and resolve to become a better person. I become not just
more able to fight temptation; my actual disposition toward sins
(of commission and omission) changes. As unbelievable as this
sounds, there have been months when I was afraid to get any-
where near past temptations. In those periods, the flaxen cords are
gone, and we are again able to use our agency to act and not be
acted upon. We can feel overwhelmed by our Heavenly Father's
love and the constant presence of the Holy Ghost, and we won't
want to lose it for a second.

The blessings from a mighty change are far-reaching. President

Benson explained, "[Those] who turn their lives over to God will find out that he can make a lot more out of their lives than they can. He will deepen their joys, expand their vision, quicken their minds, strengthen their muscles, lift their spirits, multiply their blessings, increase their opportunities, comfort their souls, raise up friends, and pour out peace."[135]

Those who receive a physical heart transplant require regular checkups to ensure that their new hearts are beating in a strong and healthy manner. Likewise, after receiving a mighty change of heart, we need to monitor our spiritual hearts to ensure that they are functioning properly.[136] Do we continue to "feel so now"? If not, there is a problem. We can know if our changed hearts are functioning properly by looking for the results described in scripture: increased revelation, love, joy, and peace.

A Mighty Change of Heart Produces Increased Revelation

Upon receiving a mighty change of heart, the desire to obey more perfectly, to align our will with God's, and to receive personal revelation all markedly increase. The change is humbling, powerful, and sweet. Remember these priceless emotions and experiences. Record them. They are miracles you cannot afford to forget.

Personal Revelation

One of the results of a changed heart includes increased personal revelation. After the Spirit "wrought a mighty change in" King Benjamin's people, they received "great views of that which is to come; and were it expedient, [they] could prophesy of all things" (Mosiah 5:2–3).

In other words, when it was needful, they could foresee the future *in all things!* Perhaps their loving Heavenly Father gave them an increased ability to make beneficial decisions because they better understood the outcomes. He is our loving Father, too. We too may receive increased prophetic revelatory power by virtue of this mighty change. Elder McConkie explained, "If all of the Latter-day Saints lived as they should, then Moses' petition [in Numbers 11:29] would be granted: 'Would God that all the Lord's people were prophets, and that the Lord would put his spirit upon them!'"[137]

Likewise, when we have frequent personal revelations, we will have particularly effective prayers because we will know for what we should be asking. The Lord told Nephi, "And now, because thou hast done this with such unwearyingness, . . . *all things shall be done unto thee according to thy word, for thou shalt not ask that which is contrary to my will*" (Helaman 10:5; emphasis added).

When our will is perfectly aligned with God's, we can in fact move mountains and command the elements. This can lead to some of the most precious miracles of our lives.

Doctrinal Revelation

A mighty change of heart also produces an increased ability to receive doctrinal revelation. When Nephi's brothers "[could] not understand the words which [their] father [the prophet] had spoken," Nephi told them that these prophetic statements would be made known "*if ye will not harden your hearts*" and ask in faith, with diligence in keeping commandments (1 Nephi 15:7–11). Alma also explained that those who harden their hearts will be "given the lesser portion of the word until they know nothing concerning his mysteries," while he who "will not harden his heart, to him is given the greater portion of the word, until it is given unto him to know the mysteries of God until he know them in full" (Alma 12:9–10).

Absent hard hearts, we can receive revelation on every point of doctrine for ourselves. The Lord declared through Joseph

Smith, "God hath not revealed anything unto Joseph, but what He will make known unto the Twelve, and even the least Saint may know all things as fast as he is able to bear them."[138] Indeed, not only will God reveal every point of doctrine to us by the power of the Holy Ghost, He *must* reveal doctrine to us each individually in order for us to reach our divine potential.

Brigham Young taught: "Now those men, or those women, who know no more about the power of God, and the influences of the Holy Spirit, than to be led entirely by another person, suspending their own understanding, and pinning their faith upon another's sleeve, will never be capable of entering into the celestial glory, to be crowned as they anticipate; they will never be capable of becoming Gods."[139]

Although we are already blessed with past and present prophets, including volumes of scripture and ongoing revelation directed toward our day, the Lord wants us to each receive personal, doctrinal revelation. In the end, we cannot simply believe the testimony of others.

Perhaps after a mighty change of heart we can become like "Nephi and Lehi, and many of their brethren who knew concerning the true points of doctrine, having many revelations daily" (Helaman 11:23). When our "new heart" is functioning properly, we should all seek for and receive this divine confirmation.

Some consider it superfluous to seek personal doctrinal revelation when we have so much past and continuing revelation. However, private doctrinal revelations are necessary because every scripture "is so written as to reveal little or much, depending on the spiritual capacity of the student."[140] Like a personal Liahona, the same scripture can also provide different meanings at different times in our lives and can even open up the doors to revelation on entirely different subjects (see Alma 37:38–46).

Because these are the last days, apostasy abounds. Nephi fore-told, "They have all gone astray save it be a few, who are the humble followers of Christ" (2 Nephi 28:14). And even these few humble Saints "in *many instances* . . . do err because they are taught by the precepts of men" (2 Nephi 28:14; emphasis added). We cannot avoid the teachings of men mingled with scripture. Comforting spins on the truth are everywhere, and they gradually bind us with Satan's flaxen cords. With a new heart that receives personal doctrinal revelation, however, we are protected by know-ing the truth of all things.

A Mighty Change of Heart Produces Increased Love, or Charity

Paul wrote to the Galatians that the "fruit of the spirit" in-cludes love, joy, and peace (Galatians 5:22). Scriptural accounts repeatedly describe this fruit as an immediate (and, ideally, last-ing) result of a mighty change of heart. Given the overwhelming presence of the Holy Spirit after receiving this change, prevalence of those fruits would be expected.

Again, after receiving "a change of heart," Alma "felt to sing the song of redeeming love" (Alma 5:26). Increased love—specifically, the "pure love of Christ," also known as charity (Moroni 7:47)—blesses your own life as well as the lives of others.

Those full of God's love cannot help but love their fellow man. After eating the fruit of the tree of life, Lehi wanted his family to join him.[141] After receiving a mighty change, Enos also was immediately full of charity. "When I had heard these words I began to feel a desire for the welfare of my brethren, the Nephites," he wrote, "wherefore, I did pour out my whole soul unto God for them" (Enos 1:9).

The sons of Mosiah had the same experience. After receiv-ing a mighty change, "they were desirous that salvation should be declared to every creature, for they could not bear that any human soul should perish" (Mosiah 28:3). In fact, these former persecutors of the Church didn't just want to serve a mission. They begged to serve in the most dangerous and challenging mission for *fourteen years!* Many years earlier, Enos described those they wanted to teach: "Their hatred was fixed, and they were led by their evil nature that they became wild, and ferocious, and a blood-thirsty people, full of idolatry and filthiness; feeding upon beasts of prey; dwelling in tents, and wandering about in the wilderness with a short skin girdle about their loins and their heads shaven; and their skill was in the bow, and in the cimeter, and the ax. And many of them did eat nothing save it was raw meat; and they were continually seeking to destroy us" (Enos 1:20).

During this mission, instead of taking one of the Lamanite king's daughters to wife (as the king offered), Ammon simply asked if he could be a servant (Alma 17:24–25). After protecting the king's flocks, Ammon taught and converted the king and his entire court. This led to a decree that Ammon and his brethren be allowed to preach in all the land. As a result of their missionary efforts, thousands of the Lamanites were brought to the truth and "the curse of God did no more follow them" (Alma 23:18)!

Alma the Younger, Peter, Paul, Enoch, the brother of Jared, and others didn't just sit at home reading scriptures after experiencing a mighty change of heart. Instead, each one of them served others with magnificent results. The stories are endless. When your heart is changed, you will be full of charity, the pure love of Christ. Your overwhelming desire to serve will bless the lives of others.

Like Faith, Charity Is a Divine Gift, Not Something We Can Attain on Our Own

The lobby of the Washington D.C. Temple contains a thirty-foot mural depicting Matthew 25:31–46, showing people throughout the ages and from all countries at Christ's Second Coming. Christ is separating those who will receive "life eternal" from those who will receive "everlasting punishment" (on his right and left sides, respectively). Many factors could be used to make this determination: church membership, meeting and temple attendance, level of faith, or—perhaps most obvious—obedience to an extensive list of commandments. The Lord chose only one qualification: charity.

To those who would return to heaven, he declared, "For I was an hungred, and ye gave me meat: I was thirsty, and ye gave me drink: I was a stranger, and ye took me in: Naked, and ye clothed me: I was sick, and ye visited me: I was in prison, and ye came unto me" (Matthew 25:35–36). It is that simple. Those who wish to save their life will lose it, and those who "lose [their] life for [His] sake shall find it" (Matthew 16:25).

Charity is essential to obtaining celestial glory. Can we, then, have charity by doing acts of charity? No.

We have all performed acts of service without being full of charity. Regardless of the good results, service performed reluctantly is worth very little. In fact, Elder Busche explained, "Serving without joyfulness . . . is an abomination in the eyes of God and will bear no fruit."[142] Deuteronomy 28:47–48 states, "Because thou servedst not the Lord thy God with joyfulness, and with gladness of heart, for the abundance of all things . . . he shall put a yoke of iron upon thy neck."[143]

Serving without joy is not charity. Receiving increased willpower to do service projects does not suffice. And you can't be full of charity without being *filled* with charity by God.

Like nearly everything of real worth, including faith and grace, charity is not something you can get on your own. While you can be receptive to receiving charity by reigning in your selfish instincts—"see that ye bridle all your passions, that ye may be filled with love," wrote Alma—being "filled with love" remains a gift (Alma 38:12).

Charity is not an activity, but a state of being given to those who "pray unto the Father with all the energy of heart" to "be filled with this love, *which he hath bestowed* upon all who are true followers of his Son, Jesus Christ" (Moroni 7:48; emphasis added). Charity is not something you can do; it is something you are given.[144]

Charity Retains a Remission of Sin

According to 1 Corinthians 13, charity is the greatest of all qualities that anyone can possess. Despite all of your other positive attributes—even faith to move mountains—"if ye have not charity, ye are nothing" (Moroni 7:46). Charity is the paradigmatic Christlike attribute, and it is essential to obtaining celestial glory. Perhaps this is why: charity retains a remission of sins in ourselves and prevents sin in others.

Joseph Smith's translation of 1 Peter 4:8 reads, "And above all things have fervent charity among yourselves; for charity preventeth a multitude of sins." When we are full of the pure love of Christ, we forsake sin. Instead of formerly enticing sins being tempting, we "look upon sin . . . with abhorrence" (Alma 13:12).

King Benjamin told his people that if they would simply care for those in need, they would "[retain] a remission of [their] sins from day to day, that [they] may walk guiltless before God" (Mosiah 4:26). This is huge! *When you perform acts of charity while being full of the pure love of Christ, you will retain a remission of your sins.*

Moreover, when we act with charity toward others, the love of Christ prevents sin in them. Joseph Smith explained: "We must be merciful to one another and overlook small things. . . .

Nothing is so much calculated to lead people to forsake sin as to take them by the hand, and watch over them with tenderness."[145]

Parents and teachers learn this same lesson by experience. As President Thomas S. Monson explained, "When we treat people merely as they are, they will remain as they are. When we treat them as if they were what they should be, they will become what they should be."[146] And when you don't look at others with charity, the pure love of Christ, you are doing them (and yourself) an immense disservice.

> When you perform acts of charity while being full of the pure love of Christ, you will retain a remission of your sins.

I've only been in one real fight, and it was with a kid in elementary school. I'll call him Trent. Trent was known by everyone as a bad kid. He said bad words, he threw things, he flipped up girls' dresses, he stole other kids' food, and he was always being sent to the principal's office. One day, our teacher asked me to hold the door open for the class when we went to recess, a privilege given to the most well-behaved student. Trent cut ahead, shoved me out of the way, and growled, "I get to hold the door."

After I disagreed and stood firmly in front of the door, he punched me. I had never been punched like that. I was shocked, and we got into a fight. We were immediately dragged by our ears to the principal's office. There, with a paddle, the principal bent Trent over the desk and counted out ten hard swats, with Trent sobbing throughout the process. I can still remember his tear-stained face. I didn't get paddled because the principal immediately took my side. As we reentered the classroom, Trent blowing his nose in a tissue, sniffling, and wiping away tears, I was congratulated. Everyone hated Trent.

But this was far from over. My mom's punishment was worse than any paddling. "You need to invite him over to play," she insisted, and there was no use arguing. The next day, I quickly asked Trent if he wanted to come over, hoping he'd say no. I was frightened that someone might notice or that Trent would make a scene.

"Sure," he said. I couldn't believe it—the horrible kid that everybody hated, the one I had been in a physical fight with—was actually coming to my house to play. That same day (without needing to call and ask permission, to my surprise), Trent put on his backpack and followed me home. I remember speed walking down the six blocks and passing through the side iron gate without going inside for my mom's usual "Hello, how was your day?" or some cookies and milk.

I set down my backpack, took off my shoes, and without even looking up, climbed onto the trampoline and started jumping. I hoped Trent would just climb onto the trampoline, jump for a few minutes, and then go home and it would all be over.

As it turned out, Trent had never been on a trampoline before. He bounced around like a headless chicken—falling down, flailing arms. I had to show him how to jump with his legs beneath him. He laughed and laughed, and I showed him how to bounce on your knees and back to your feet, how to bounce on your back, how to "double bounce" someone by jumping immediately before they land. With a child's ability to forget, I too was soon laughing.

After no more than ten minutes, however, Trent, started crying. He collapsed onto the trampoline, legs crossed, head in his hands.

"What's wrong?" I asked, oblivious.

"I . . . I finally have a friend, and now . . . I have to go," he sobbed.

I could hardly understand him. "What do you mean?" I asked. "Where?"

"I have to move to Arizona and live with my grandma," Trent said. "My dad left my mom and me, so Mom started drinking, and she got a bubble in her brain. . . . Last week, the bubble broke and she died. So now I have to live with my grandma."

I saw Trent for less than a week before he went to Arizona.

I would love to know what happened to him, if he remained the "bad kid," if he went to college, if he's in prison somewhere, or if he's raising a beautiful family. I don't know whether his life got worse or better, but I will never forget what happened to me. If we are able to see others with the pure love of Christ, we can recognize those who are suffering without judging them first. I was so wrong to dislike Trent when I had no idea what he was going through. I never want to make that mistake again.

As Latter-day Saints, we have so many commandments and rules that at times we can feel overwhelmed or our motivations can get clouded. Some of us are so busy juggling priorities in our lives that we miss the big picture. So, like the Pharisee asking which commandment was the most important, we too could use reminding: love God, and love your neighbor like yourself (see Matthew 22:37–40). As President Dieter F. Uchtdorf explained, love is the "constant compass that can help us prioritize our lives, thoughts, and actions . . . [and] ought to be at the *center* of all and everything we do in our own family, in our Church callings, and in our livelihood."[147]

Receiving and retaining charity, the pure love of Christ, may be the most valuable gift that accompanies a changed heart.

Indeed, being filled with the love of Christ serves as our protection from sin. *A mighty change of heart will not make you sinless, but it ought to make you sin less.*

A Mighty Change of Heart Produces Increased— and Exceeding—Joy

Blast this Christmas music! It's joyful and triumphant.
—How the Grinch Stole Christmas[148]

After considering different Halloween costumes—the front-runner being "pizza"—our son Max asked with a furrowed brow, "Why is Christmas better than Halloween? Did Jesus make that happen?"

Yes, Jesus made that happen. Despite its commercial trappings, for me Christmas is hands down the best holiday because it is a time of joy. When Jesus was born, an angel declared, "Fear not: for, behold, I bring you tidings of great joy, which shall be to all people" (Luke 2:10). And with hot chocolate in hand, we belt "Joy to the World" at the top of our lungs.

Along with increased spiritual power, personal revelation, and charity, a mighty change of heart produces increased joy. "Joy is more than happiness," Elder Dallin H. Oaks explained. "Joy is the ultimate sensation of well-being."[149] Scriptures describe an "exceeding joy," a "joy which none receiveth save it be the truly penitent and humble seeker of happiness" (Alma 27:18).

Alma received this exceeding joy when he had a mighty change of heart, finally cleansed from years of painful sin. He proclaimed, "Oh, what joy, and what marvelous light I did behold; yea, my soul was filled with joy as exceeding as was my pain!" (Alma 36:20).

Mankind has always sought exceeding joy. When King Benjamin asked his people to take those steps that lead to a mighty change, he suggested they "consider . . . the happy state of those that keep the commandments" (Mosiah 2:41). And after "the Spirit of the Lord Omnipotent, . . . wrought a mighty change in [the people of King Benjamin], or in [their] hearts . . . they did rejoice with such exceedingly great joy" (Mosiah 5:2, 4).[150]

> A mighty change of heart will not make you sinless, but it ought to make you sin less.

After Aaron taught the gospel to the king over all the Lamanites, the king volunteered to "give up all that [he] possess[ed]," even forsaking his kingdom to "receive this great joy" (Alma 22:15). Like modern celebrities and multimillionaires, the king seemingly had it all. But what he didn't have was exceeding joy. He realized that the joy that comes from a mighty change of heart was better than everything he had, and worth trading all of his possessions for.

Exceedingly Great Joy Is the Purpose of Life

We all seek joy as if it were the purpose of life because it is. President David O. McKay taught that "happiness is the purpose and design of existence,"[151] and the gospel is "the great plan of happiness" (Alma 42:8). All of Christ's teachings exist, the Savior explained, "that [His] joy might remain in you, and that your joy might be full" (John 15:11). In His "presence is fulness of joy" (Psalm 16:11), and seeking and receiving that joy is the purpose of this life. Indeed, "men *are,* that they might have joy" (2 Nephi 2:25, emphasis added).

It is the innate search for joy itself that, when unmet, leads to false and unfulfilling substitutes. Thomas Aquinas, a prominent medieval Christian theologian and philosopher, wrote, "Man cannot live without joy; therefore when he is deprived of true spiritual joys it is necessary that he become addicted to carnal pleasures."[152]

Satan knows this. Just as the Father and Son's plan is for us to experience joy, the deceiver wants the opposite. "Because he had fallen from heaven, and had become miserable forever, [Satan] sought also the misery of all mankind" (2 Nephi 2:18). When our hearts harden and Satan binds us in his flaxen cords, we too find ourselves in "a state of misery and endless torment" (Mosiah 3:25), and "misery shall be [our] doom" (Moses 7:37).

As one author put it, if you seek happiness by focusing on "body and beauty and sexual allure . . . you will always feel ugly. And when time and age start showing, you will die a million deaths before they finally grieve you. . . . Worship power, you will end up feeling weak and afraid, and you will need ever more power over others to numb you to your own fear. Worship your intellect, being seen as smart, you will end up feeling stupid, a fraud, always on the verge of being found out."[153]

It's true: pursuing things like sex, money, power, or drug-induced euphoria may bring temporary pleasure. But the pursuit of temporary pleasure doesn't lead to lasting happiness or joy. As my drug addict friend Joey found out, obtaining pleasure from a repeated sin requires you to engage in that activity more and more just to feel normal, and ultimately, you will feel nothing but terrible and empty. Those who remain on Satan's path will inevitably "remain with the father of lies, in misery, like unto himself" (2 Nephi 9:9).

As humbling and difficult as submitting to God's will can feel, it is ultimately the only way to find exceeding joy—the very purpose and design of our existence.

We Can Have Joy amid Adversity

A life of joy is not necessarily a life without trials. Since Adam and Eve left Eden, we face a telestial world filled with thorns and must survive by the sweat of aging, imperfect bodies. Although much of life's adversity results from our own choices, we cannot avoid trials even if we live righteous lives.

However, having trials does not mean that we will experience any less joy. In fact, we can have exceeding joy amid affliction just as easily as someone can experience misery amid wealth and ease.[154] Paul wrote, "I am exceeding joyful in all our tribulation" (2 Corinthians 7:4).

When we receive and maintain a mighty change of heart, when we have the Lord's Spirit as our guide and comforter, He will ensure our greatest happiness. Remember, it is not some things but "all things [that] work together for good to them that love God" (Romans 8:28). With an all-powerful God on our side, we can stand in the hottest fire and not be burned or in a pit of lions and not be eaten (see Daniel 3, 6).

When our hearts are receptive to the Lord's will, we will have exceeding joy regardless of our trials and the circumstances of our lives. Elder Richard G. Scott explained, "When you trust in the Lord, when you are willing to let your heart and your mind be centered in His will, when you ask to be led by the Spirit to do His will, *you are assured of the greatest happiness along the way* and the most fulfilling attainment from this mortal experience."[155]

> We all seek joy as if it were the purpose of life because *it is*.

We are supposed to be happy. We are supposed to have exceeding joy. And we receive (and maintain) this joy—regardless of adversity—through a mighty change of heart.

A Mighty Change of Heart Produces Increased Peace

"These things I have spoken unto you," Christ told His Apostles, "that in me ye might have peace" (John 16:33). After He was crucified and then resurrected, His first message was

"Peace be unto you" (John 20:21). Indeed, our Savior is "The Prince of Peace" (Isaiah 9:6).

Therefore, as we become more Christlike, increased peace results from a mighty change of heart. After "the Spirit of the Lord came upon [King Benjamin's people], and they were filled with joy" they received "peace of conscience" (Mosiah 4:3). Peace of conscience is a precious blessing. As the French proverb goes, "There is no pillow so soft as a clear conscience." My grandfather used to say the reason he was able to immediately fall asleep was a clear conscience, and I believed him.

We all have experienced the anxiety, heartache, and painful consequences of repeated sin. Surely, each of us has at one time felt "wretched," "sorrow[ing] because of [our] flesh" and "griev[ing] because of [our] iniquities" (2 Nephi 4: 17–20). The blessing of having the Lord "remember [our sins] no more" is amazing, indeed (D&C 58:42).

However, Christ's peace is even greater than what the world calls a "clear conscience." His peace provides comfort for this life as well as the life to come. When we trust in Him (i.e., have firm faith) as opposed to our short-sighted eyes and weak arms of flesh, we receive peaceful confirmation that our best interests will come to pass.

Isaiah wrote, "Thou wilt keep him in perfect peace, whose mind is stayed on thee: because he trusteth in thee" (Isaiah 26:3). This "perfect peace" trumps any natural physiological counterpart. Perfect peace is a firm and lasting "peace of God, which passeth all understanding" (Philippians 4:7). This exceeds our understanding because we can feel it despite apparent contradictions. Joseph Smith recorded such peace, for example, when he went to his death "like a lamb to the slaughter; but . . . calm as a summer's morning" (D&C 135:4).

Christ's peace also exceeds our understanding because it is more powerful and lasting than any mortal peace we could experience. Surpassing the world's greatest anti-anxiety medication or fear-fighting practice, Christ is "the only source of enduring peace."[156] During the last supper, Christ told His disciples: "Peace I leave with you, *my* peace I give unto you: *not as the world giveth,* give I unto you. Let not your heart be troubled, neither let it be afraid" (John 14:27; emphasis added).

With His perfect peace, we don't need to be afraid or worry. Our life is in the hands of a benevolent Father who is all powerful and all knowing. His "covenant of peace" with us is His way of letting us know that He is directing our lives (Ezekiel 37:26). Peace confirms that it is His voice that guides us when our mortal eyes cannot see. "Did I not speak peace to your mind concerning the matter?" the Savior asked Oliver Cowdery. "What greater witness can you have than from God?" (D&C 6:23).

Moreover, because the Lord's peace is not as the world gives, neither Satan nor anything in this world can replicate it. Creature comforts are a pitiful substitute. Remember, sometimes we have no clue what is in our best interest. We could seek comfort in the decision to buy a home, for example, by purchasing insurance, but that home might end up with termite damage that isn't covered. We could choose a job that seems perfect only to have the factory close or the career become outdated. We could move to a city that later has an earthquake, or get hit by a car on the way to the grocery store, or

> When you ask to be led by the Spirit to do the Lord's will, you are assured of the greatest happiness along the way.

invest our retirement money in a business that turns out to be a scam.

Following God's peaceful guidance, we can find the path that will bring us the greatest happiness. And if that path is bumpy, God can ensure that we experience joy despite the trials.

The introduction to the Book of Mormon states: "The crowning event recorded in the Book of Mormon is the personal ministry of the Lord Jesus Christ among the Nephites soon after His resurrection. It puts forth the doctrines of the gospel, outlines the plan of salvation, and *tells men what they must do to gain peace in this life* and eternal salvation in the life to come" (emphasis added). The Prince of Peace lived, taught, and died so that we may gain peace in *this life,* not just in the life to come. His exceeding, perfect peace is another precious gift of the Spirit we receive after experiencing a mighty change of heart.

KEY POINTS

THE FRUITS OF A MIGHTY CHANGE

Some miraculous results of a mighty change of heart include the following:

1. Increased revelation—personal and doctrinal.

2. Increased charity (the pure love of Christ). Like faith, charity is a gift, not something we can attain on our own. It prevents sin in ourselves, retains a remission of sin, and helps others to not sin.

3. Increased joy—having exceeding joy is the purpose of life, and we can have joy amid adversity. We can be assured that all things are for our good.

4. Increased peace—we can receive peace of conscience, which surpasses understanding, and receive peace that removes fear and worry, knowing that God directs everything to our greatest joy and benefit.

CONCLUSION

The scriptures could not be more clear. Our Savior's plan is not just about getting back to heaven; He wants us to be happy in this life. He wants us to be full of His love, His exceeding joy, and His perfect peace *now*. In fact, happiness is the purpose of our existence.

To receive His love, joy, and peace, however, we cannot repeatedly commit the same sins. Repetitive, unrepented sin is not compatible with our Savior's most fulfilling gifts. We all must ultimately learn this lesson—sometimes more than once. In short, we need to decide which we want more: fleeting pleasures that ultimately don't satisfy or Christ's love, joy, and peace. This is the fundamental question.

At times, perhaps we have figured we could have a bit of both—that left foot in Zion and the right in Babylon. We have given in to various temptations because they were, after all, tempting. Perhaps we were simply curious or trying to fit in. We thought we'd be okay "committing a little sin" (nobody needs to know) and then stopping if and when the short-term pleasure wasn't worth the pain (2 Nephi 28:8).

But we were wrong. You and I have been wrong over and over. It's a "false and vain and foolish doctrine" (2 Nephi 28:9). Choices to pit our will against God's allow Satan to ensnare us with sin's initially imperceptible flaxen cords. We don't want to feel the pangs of the Holy Spirit and, as a result, our hearts harden. Then, when our hearts stop functioning properly, we cannot feel the Spirit like we should. We can't hear our Father's voice or feel His hand guiding us through the darkness. If we become full of pride and Satan's lies, we may procrastinate repentance too long, and our agency can become fatally compromised.

Each one of us has spent too much time with diminished agency, spiritually weak and in personal cycles of sin. We have followed that downhill road that wasn't too straight but was plenty broad. Passing fellow travelers, we figured we were heading somewhere fine enough. Of course, we weren't.

With hard hearts, it isn't easy to know what we want the most. We can't remember that the Lord's peace and joy feel infinitely better than a one-hour buzz, a thirty-second rush, or five seconds of pleasure. "Great faith has a short shelf life," as President Henry B. Eyring put it,[157] and like the Nephites, we are just too quick to forget.

Fortunately, we have also all experienced the flipside of this cycle. At some point, while reading a scripture or giving food to the homeless or hearing loving counsel, our stony hearts have been touched. Frustrated with our lives of repetitive sin, we have felt humble. Perhaps the Lord loved us so much that He helped us in that humbling process. He let us face the painful consequences of sin, the trials of poverty, illness, or natural disasters. It is in those times that we finally want to change. For a time, we realize that no man can have two masters, and we want to be on the winning team for good.

We have all been there. Each one of us has sins (of commission and omission) that, for one reason or another, we have not yet been able to fully shake—we can't get ourselves "unstuck." Yet many of us have wanted to make that permanent change, to quit those repetitive sins once and for all.

So here's the million dollar question: How do you do it? *You* don't.

The question isn't how you can overcome cycles of sin, let alone return to heaven, because, ultimately, *you can't.* Maybe you have the wherewithal to overcome the occasional routine temptation. But when it comes to the big battles—our own individually tailored, repetitive sins—we are all too weak.

And we are *supposed* to be too weak! God gave us weakness! He placed us in a fallen world. He gave us weakness so that we would be humble. Like Gideon's army, we cannot win life's battles on our own. We cannot just rally up our discipline and "1-2-3-repent." Instead, we need "faith unto repentance." And we can't just "have faith" unto repentance, because we need to be *given* faith. We can't just "have charity," either. It is *Christ's* pure love; it is *His* gift to give.

So, to clarify, focusing on willpower is both useful and dangerous. Willpower and discipline are hallmarks of a faithful path. Yet we must ensure that dwelling on our own ability to obey does not prevent a humble recognition of our ultimate inability. Focusing on personal righteousness should never overshadow the truth that "our righteousnesses are as filthy rags" (Isaiah 64:6) and that we cannot overcome repetitive sin alone. Overcoming sins requires the Lord's grace, His enabling strength. We need His mighty change of heart.

The mighty change of heart and its accompanying blessings are divine gifts that are ours for the taking. The Savior's hand is outstretched. We just need to want it.

We need to want Him to be the gardener and to use His pruning shears as He sees fit. We need to throw away that "just in case" package of cigarettes. We need to be so humble that we can finally, decisively, and unfalteringly decide. After all, if you don't really want the Lord to grant this mighty change of heart, He won't. He cannot, because our hard-fought agency is too precious.

I know many of us have had a hard time trusting our own resolve. We've tried to repent and returned to our "favorite sins" over and over. But Christ extends His hand of mercy further still. If we can just be *honest* with Him—no more hiding, no more secrecy—and ask in complete sincerity, He will strengthen our resolve. After all, faith is a gift.

Sadly, with repetitive sin, we can become so used to secrecy that we aren't even honest with ourselves. Perhaps we need to wrestle with God, and that's okay. Discover your true intentions. *Own your hard-fought agency.* If you find it hard to place your trust in Him and to stop relying on your own arm of flesh, admit it! He already knows. There is no benefit in rationalizing or pretending. God knows what we've done, and He knows why we did it. We might as well decide to be honest with Him and speed up the process of receiving His grace.

Remember, if you had the strength or willpower on your own, you would not repeatedly commit the same sins or fail to make lasting change. You know that the Lord's joy, His love, and His peace outweigh worldly substitutes. There is no question whether His all-knowing plan for our personal happiness in this life (let alone the life to come) is greater than anything we can conceive of. We know this. We just need to sincerely ask Him to help strengthen our resolve.

We also need to remember the scriptural guides to maintaining a mighty change of heart. We must avoid proximity to sins we find most tempting and escape the instant temptation arises. Although our Father prepared a way to avoid sin, we have to remember that waiting too long before jumping ship isn't it.

Moreover, although we ought to fear those sins that we find most tempting, we can't dwell on them. We have to stop focusing on avoiding temptation. Instead of focusing on our specific weaknesses, we need center our thoughts on Christ. When we focus on Christ, our desires and motivations center on doing good, and doing so continually. We need to replace hours once lost to sin and hiding with activities that make us better people and allow us to bless the lives of others. Once you experience a mighty change of heart, it's amazing how much time you have to spend in beneficial ways.

After receiving a mighty change of heart, we still must be continuous in our efforts, because we are so quick to forget. Unless we are exercising continual efforts for good, before long we will yet again overestimate our ability to fight temptation. We need to pray all the time. We need to repent immediately and continually. We cannot allow ourselves to live for any period of time without the companionship of the Holy Spirit.

Finally, being aware of all of the results of a mighty change can help us monitor our hearts for continued spiritual receptiveness. Some gifts that accompany a change of heart include increased revelation (personal and doctrinal); increased charity (being full of Christ's love); exceeding joy (which can exist amid adversity); and receiving the Lord's peace, which assures us everything will be for our good in a way

> Own your hard-fought agency.

that surpasses mortal understanding. As we look for and recognize these spiritual gifts in our lives, we can receive the confirmation that we are continually "feel[ing] so now."

This may be the most powerful truth in the universe: "All things work together for good to them that love God" (Romans 8:28). Do you love Him? It doesn't matter what you did or didn't do or how many times you did it. So what if you can't seem to change your habitual behavior? It may be true that you can't stop committing those sins you once enjoyed, because you can't change your own hardened heart. But *He can.*

You just need to want it. It is literally that simple. So, be honest. Do you?

NOTES

1. We are also equally blameworthy and in need of the Savior's Atonement. As James wrote, "For whosoever shall keep the whole law, and yet offend in one point, he is guilty of all" (James 2:10).
2. LDS.org, Gospel Topics, "Repentance."
3. See Moroni 8:8.
4. See Dale G. Renlund, "Preserving the Heart's Mighty Change," *Ensign*, Nov. 2009; see also Alma 7:14; Moses 6:59.
5. See Moroni 7:16–19.
6. An online search for "statistics on pornography addiction" found studies showing that 68% of young adult men view pornography at least *once a week* (see http://www.covenanteyes.com/pornstats/). Ironically, even using those well-intended search terms, a string of pornographic videos showed up on the second page of my results.
7. *Decisions for Successful Living*, Salt Lake City: Deseret Book Co. (1973), 87–88.
8. Dallin H. Oaks, "Joy and Mercy," *Ensign*, Nov. 1991, 73–75.
9. Ezra Taft Benson, "Beware of Pride," *Ensign*, May 1989, 4–7.
10. Ibid.
11. Ezra Taft Benson, "The Book of Mormon—Keystone of Our Religion," *Ensign*, Nov. 1986, 4–7.
12. See Dallin H. Oaks, "Our Strengths Can Become Our Downfall," *Ensign*, Oct. 1994, 11–19.
13. Ibid.
14. F. Enzio Busche, "Unleashing the Dormant Spirit," May 14, 1996, BYU Devotional.
15. See also Helaman 10:13.
16. Harold B. Lee, "The Message," *New Era*, Jan. 1971, 6.
17. Neal A. Maxwell, "The Education of Our Desires" (University of Utah Institute of Religion Devotional, January 5, 1983).
18. James E. Talmage, *Articles of Faith*, (1971), 119

19. See John 8:44.

20. Gordon B. Hinckley, "The Quest for Excellence," *BYU Speeches* (Nov. 10, 1998).

21. Ezra Taft Benson, "A Mighty Change of Heart," *Ensign*, Oct. 1989, 2–5.

22. Brad Wilcox, *The Continuous Atonement* (Salt Lake City: Deseret Book, 2009), 19.

23. See Neal A. Maxwell, *All These Things Shall Give Thee Experience* (Salt Lake City: Deseret Book, 1980), 31.

24. Letters edited for typographical errors.

25. Ralph Parlette, quoted by Spencer W. Kimball, *The Miracle of Forgiveness* (Salt Lake City: Bookcraft, Inc.,1969), 164.

26. Neal A. Maxwell, "If Thou Endure It Well," BYU Fireside, December 4, 1984.

27. Quoted by Donald L. Staheli, "Obedience—Life's Great Challenge," *Ensign*, May 1998, 82.

28. David A. Bednar, "In the Strength of the Lord," *Ensign*, Nov. 2004, 16–19.

29. *History of the Church*, 4:461.

30. Joseph Smith, *The Joseph Smith Papers: Histories, Volume 1: Joseph Smith Histories, 1832–1844*, ed. Karen Lynn Davidson et al. (Salt Lake City: Church Historian's Press, 2012), 11.

31. "Last Testimony of Sister Emma," *Saints' Herald 26* (October 1, 1879), 290.

32. Bruce R. McConkie, "Joseph Smith—The Mighty Prophet of the Restoration," *Ensign*, May 1976, 94–97.

33. Jeffrey R. Holland, *Christ and the New Covenant: The Messianic Message of the Book of Mormon* (1997), 17.

34. Ibid.

35. *Teachings of the Presidents of the Church: Ezra Taft Benson* (2014), 84.

36. Dale G. Renlund, "Preserving the Heart's Mighty Change," *Ensign*, Nov. 2009, 97–99.

37. James L. Ferrell, *Falling to Heaven: The Surprising Path to Happiness* (Salt Lake City: Deseret Book, 2012), 43.

38. David A. Bednar, "Clean Hands and a Pure Heart," *Ensign*, Nov. 2007, 80–83.

39. Charles Dickens, *A Christmas Carol,* chapter 1.

40. See Thomas S. Monson, "Now Is the Time," *Ensign*, Nov. 2001, 59–61.

41. *A Christmas Carol*, chapter 5.

42. M. Russell Ballard, "Be Strong in the Lord," *Ensign*, July 2004, 11–12.

43. The second single from DJ Jazzy Jeff & The Fresh Prince's album *He's the DJ, I'm the Rapper.*

44. George Q. Cannon, Discourse at Temple Square (November 27, 1864), found in *Journal of Discourses*, 11:47. See also Richard G. Scott, "The Atonement Can Secure Your Peace and Happiness," *Ensign*, Nov. 2006, 40–42.

45. L. Tom Perry, "Obedience through Our Faithfulness," *Ensign*, May 2014, 100–103.

46. M. Russell Ballard, "Be Strong in the Lord," *Ensign*, July 2004, 11–12.

47. Humbly confessing one's captivity is the first step in any recovery program (e.g., Alcoholics Anonymous or the Church's Addiction Recovery Program)—admitting you are "powerless over" a given compulsive behavior or sin (see Alcoholics Anonymous, "Chapter 5: How It Works" [4th ed., June 2001]; see also *Addiction Recovery Program: A Guide to Addiction Recovery and Healing*, iv, 1–5).

48. *The American Heritage® Dictionary of the English Language*, Fifth Edition (2014), Houghton Mifflin Harcourt Publishing Company.

49. Poverty is not inevitably linked with misery any more than wealth is always accompanied by happiness. The greatest joys and happiness come from following a path ordained by God. To the extent that riches lead to pride and trusting the arm of flesh, they will inevitably produce greater bondage and heartache.

50. Gordon B. Hinckley, *Standing for Something: 10 Neglected Virtues That Will Heal Our Hearts and Homes*, (New York: Three Rivers Press, 2000), 129.

51. David A. Bednar, "Clean Hands and a Pure Heart," *Ensign*, Nov. 2007, 80–83; emphasis added.

52. Gospel Topics, LDS.org, "Faith."

53. BibleStudyTools.com, s.v. "Pistis," KJV New Testament Greek Lexicon.

54. "Faith," Merriam-Webster.com. 2015. http://www.merriam-webster.com /dictionary/faith (June 5, 2015).

55. We cannot trust any man's "arm of flesh," including our own. If we base religious decisions on any person's persuasive argument, we will always find someone else with new "facts" and a different and more effective

spin. This is why Christ told Peter he was "blessed"—because his faith in the Savior came from his "Father which is in heaven" and that "flesh and blood" (Matthew 16:17).

56. Henry B. Eyring, "In the Strength of the Lord," *Ensign*, May 2004, 16–19.

57. *Collins English Dictionary*, HarperCollins Publishers (2015).

58. Bible Dictionary, s.v. "Grace."

59. "Metanoia," Merriam-Webster.com. 2015. http://www.merriam-webster .com/dictionary/metanoia (June 5, 2015).

60. As a semantic point, one may argue an exception here if praying for the gift of faith constitutes "work." Obedience also may result in obtaining additional faith, but only when coupled with grace (another gift). A focus on our own disciplined obedience as opposed to His enabling gifts of grace and faith will not suffice. Moreover, this focus can ultimately hinder our salvation when it produces more trust in the arm of flesh and less in broken-hearted humility.

61. See also Brad Wilcox, *The Continuous Atonement*, 104 ("The word *after* could also be read as *in spite of*. We are saved by grace in spite of all we can do.") (Salt Lake City: Deseret Book, 2009).

62. James E. Talmage, *Articles of Faith*, (1984), 111; emphasis added.

63. The Guide to the Scriptures, "veil."

64. Quoting Harold B. Lee, in "The Edge of the Light," *BYU Magazine* (March 1991).

65. Gerald N. Lund, "Salvation: By Grace or by Works?" *Ensign*, Apr. 1981, 16–23.

66. Joseph Smith, *Lectures on Faith*, Deseret Book (1985), 46.

67. See also Joseph Fielding McConkie, Robert L. Millet, *The Holy Ghost* (Bookcraft 1989), 105, quoting *By Grace Are We Saved*, 54–55 ("To be sanctified in regard to vice is to shudder and shake at its appearance, to feel a revulsion for whatever allurements would detour or detain the human heart").

68. William Law, *A Serious Call to a Devout and Holy Life* (London: J. M. Dent; New York: E. P. Dutton, 1920), 13.

69. *The Edge of the Sword* (London: Faber & Faber, 1960), 117–18.

70. James E. Talmage, *The Articles of Faith*, 111.

71. Hugh B. Brown, "The Currant Bush," *New Era*, Jan. 1973.

72. Ibid.

73. Ibid.

74. Jeffrey R. Holland, "For Times of Trouble," BYU Devotional Address (March 1980); emphasis added.

75. Mark Twain, *The Adventures of Huckleberry Finn*, chapter 31.

76. Michael McCarthy, "Vegas Goes Back to Naughty Roots," *USA Today*, April 11, 2005.

77. See also James E. Faust, "The Enemy Within," *Ensign*, Nov. 2000. ("Some people wear masks of decency and outward righteousness but live lives of deception, believing that, like Dr. Jekyll, they can live a double life and never be found out.")

78. Spencer W. Kimball, *The Miracle of Forgiveness* (Salt Lake City: Bookcraft, 1989), 110.

79. "In Memoriam A. H. H." in section XCVI (96), 1849.

80. See also Mormon 9:4 ("Behold, I say unto you that ye would be more miserable to dwell with a holy and just God, under a consciousness of your filthiness before him, than ye would to dwell with the damned souls in hell").

81. David A. Bednar, "Clean Hands and a Pure Heart," *Ensign*, Nov. 2007, 80–83.

82. Ibid.; emphasis added.

83. See "Singing the Song of Redeeming Love," Joseph Walker, *Ensign*, Mar. 1993, 56–60. ("Bishops often encounter people who are willing to confess their sins but who aren't willing to make a commitment to change their behavior. 'I know what I did was wrong,' one young man told his bishop. 'But I'd be lying if I told you that I don't want to ever do it again. In fact, if I'm ever in that situation again, I'll probably do the same thing.'")

84. Neal A. Maxwell, "Swallowed up in the Will of the Father," *Ensign*, Nov. 1995, 22–24.

85. Spencer J. Condie, *In Perfect Balance* (Salt Lake City: Bookcraft, 1993), 116.

86. David A. Bednar, "Clean Hands and a Pure Heart," *Ensign*, Nov. 2007, 80–83.

87. *Oxford Dictionary*.

88. Ibid.

89. See also Brad Wilcox, *The Continuous Atonement* (Salt Lake City: Deseret Book, 2009), 171. ("Does this mean that they never made another mistake

or had another bad day? No. They probably messed up just like we do, since they were living in the same fallen world in which we live. The issue isn't whether or not they slipped but that they didn't want to . . . They lived in a constant spirit of repentance because of their righteous desires.")

90. Brent W. Webb, "Repentance: A Mighty Change of Heart," BYU Devotional (May 18, 1999).

91. Although the "boiling frog" experiments in 1872 and 1875 have been recently disproven, the metaphor still illustrates a true principle. Whit Gibbons, "The Legend of the Boiling Frog is Just a Legend," Savanna River Ecology Laboratory (December 23, 2007).

92. F. Enzio Busche, "Unleashing the Dormant Spirit," BYU Devotional (May 1996).

93. Boyd K. Packer, "Spiritual Crocodiles," *Ensign*, May 1976, 30–32.

94. "It is entirely possible that this interesting incident could have served as the source of the 'bury-the-hatchet' tradition of showing peace, which was a common practice among some of the tribes of American Indians when Columbus and other white men came to their lands" (Daniel Ludlow, *A Companion to Your Study of the Book of Mormon* [Salt Lake City: Deseret Book, 1976], 210).

95. David O. McKay, *Gospel Ideals* (Salt Lake City: Deseret News Press, 1953), 512.

96. The Book of Mormon also affirms that "the Lord giveth no commandments unto the children of men, save he shall prepare a way for them that they may accomplish the thing which he commandeth them" (1 Nephi 3:7; emphasis added). To emphasize that not every way will suffice, it took Nephi and his brothers three attempts in order to follow the Lord's commandment to obtain Laban's plates. Their lives were endangered twice when Laban and his men tried to kill them, and they lost "gold, and . . . silver, and all [their] precious things" in the process (1 Nephi 3:24). Despite their intents and persistence, only when they followed a course specifically inspired by the Lord (killing Laban) were they "given . . . power whereby they could accomplish the thing which the Lord hath commanded them" (1 Nephi 5:8).

97. Spencer W. Kimball, *The Miracle of Forgiveness* (Salt Lake City: Bookcraft, 1989), 114; see also Bruce R. McConkie, "Think on These Things," *Ensign*, Jan. 1974, 45–48.

98. Mark Chamberlain, "More than Willpower: How to Overcome a Destructive Habit," *Meridian Magazine* (April 15, 2004).

99. Bruce Fordham, "Think About What You Are Thinking About," *Ensign*, April 2009, 68–69.

100. See Moses 4:3.

101. *Teachings of the Presidents of the Church: David O. McKay*, (Salt Lake City: The Church of Jesus Christ of Latter-day Saints, 2003), 208.

102. "I Need Thee Every Hour," *Hymns* (1985), no. 98.

103. For those who are interested in the details, Alma's entire chiasmus from Alma chapter 36 can be outlined as follows:

a—My son, give ear to my WORDS (v. 1)

  b—KEEP THE COMMANDMENTS and ye shall PROSPER IN THE LAND (v. 1)

    c—DO AS I HAVE DONE (v. 2)

      d—in REMEMBERING THE CAPTIVITY of our fathers (v. 2)

        e—for they were in BONDAGE (v. 2)

          f—he surely did DELIVER them (v. 2)

            g—TRUST in God (v. 3)

              h—supported in their TRIALS, and TROUBLES, and AFFLICTIONS (v. 3)

                i—shall be LIFTED UP at the LAST DAY (v. 3)

                  j—I KNOW this NOT OF MYSELF but of GOD (v. 4)

                    k—BORN OF GOD (v. 5)

                      l—I SOUGHT to destroy the church of God (v. 6–9)

                        m—MY LIMBS were paralyzed (v. 10)

                          n—Fear of being in the PRESENCE OF GOD (v. 14–15)

                            o—PAINS of a damned soul (v. 16)

                              p—HARROWED UP BY THE MEMORY OF SINS (v. 17)

                                q—I remembered JESUS CHRIST, SON OF GOD (v. 17)

q—I cried, JESUS, SON OF
GOD (v. 18)

p—HARROWED UP BY THE
MEMORY OF SINS no more
(v. 19)

o—Joy as exceeding as was the PAIN
(v. 20)

n—Long to be in the PRESENCE OF
GOD (v. 22)

m—My LIMBS received their strength
again (v. 23)

l—I LABORED to bring souls to repentance
(v. 24)

k—BORN OF GOD (v. 26)

j—Therefore MY KNOWLEDGE IS OF GOD
(v. 26)

h—Supported under TRIALS, TROUBLES, and
AFFLICTIONS (v. 27)

g—TRUST in him (v. 27)

f—He will DELIVER me (v. 27)

i—and RAISE ME UP at the LAST DAY (v. 28)

e—As God brought our fathers out of BONDAGE and
captivity (v. 28–29)

d—Retain in REMEMBRANCE THEIR CAPTIVITY
(v. 28–29)

c—KNOW AS I DO KNOW (v. 30)

b—KEEP THE COMMANDMENTS and ye shall PROSPER IN
THE LAND (v. 30)

a—This is according to his WORD (v. 30)

104. See also Robert L. Millet, *Grace Works* (Salt Lake City: Deseret Book, 89–90). ("There is a better and higher motivation . . . that is above and beyond self-discipline, well beyond sheer willpower and dogged determination. It is a motivation born of the Spirit, one that comes to us as a result of a change of heart.")

105. "The Book of Mormon—Keystone of Our Religion," *Ensign*, Nov. 1986, 4–7; emphasis added.

106. *History of the Church*, 6:252; see also *History of the Church*, 3:395–96 (Brigham Young said "no man's opinion is worth a straw").

107. Hugh Nibley, *The World and the Prophets* (Salt Lake City: Deseret Book and FARMS, 1987), 134.

108. Gordon B. Hinckley, "Life's Obligations," *Ensign*, Feb. 1999, 2–5.

109. *Journal of Discourses*, 2:93–94.

110. *Journal of Discourses*, 14:210; see also D&C 88:78–80.

111. *Journal of Discourses*, 11:328. Apparently frustrated with this lack, on one occasion, the Prophet said, "In things pertaining to this life, the lack of knowledge manifested by us as a people is disgraceful. . . . I have seen months and months in this city when I could have wept like a whipped child to see the awful stupidity of the people" (JD, 11:105; 2:280).

112. *Journal of Discourses*, 13:260; see also D&C 130:18–19; 2 Nephi 9:29 ("to be learned is good if [we] hearken unto the counsels of God").

113. Gordon B. Hinckley, "A Prophet's Counsel and Prayer for Youth," *Ensign*, Jan. 2001, 2–11.

114. For example, more people die from pill overdoses or diabetes in Utah than almost any other state in the U.S.

115. Jörg Klebingat, "Approaching the Throne of God with Confidence," *Ensign*, Nov. 2014, 34–37.

116. Rex D. Pinegar, "The Simple Things," *Ensign*, Nov. 1994, 80–82.

117. "Wisdom and Order," *Ensign*, June 1994, 40–43.

118. "Take Especial Care of Your Family," *Ensign*, May 1994, 90.

119. See also Alma 31:10; Alma 37:36–37.

120. "Lord, I Would Follow Thee," *Hymns* (1985), no. 220.

121. *Approaching Zion* (Salt Lake City: Deseret Book; Provo: FARMS, 1989), 301–302.

122. David W. Hellem, "Putting Off the Natural Man: How to be 'Spiritually Born of God,'" *Ensign*, June 1992, 6–9.

123. Eric A. Eliason, *The J. Golden Kimball Stories* (Urbana-Champaign: University of Illinois Press, 2007),107; see also D&C 109:21 ("when thy people transgress, any of them, they may speedily repent and return unto thee").

124. Jörg Klebingat, "Approaching the Throne of God with Confidence," *Ensign*, Nov. 2014, 34–37.

125. Brigham Young, *Journal of Discourses*, 12:103.

126. James E. Talmage, *Articles of Faith*, (Salt Lake City: Deseret Book), 114.

127. For these purposes, a distinction may not be needed. Personally, I think guilt is not useful because it primarily makes you feel horrible about yourself, whereas godly sorrow is the emotion that motivates you to seek repentance. See 2 Corinthians 7:9–10 ("For godly sorrow worketh repentance to salvation not to be repented of: but the sorrow of the world worketh death"). Unlike godly sorrow, guilt also may occur regardless of whether someone is actually sinning. Some people may feel guilty skipping the gym one night. I feel guilty spending $60 on a haircut. Just because you feel guilty (often triggered by the superego and cultural expectations) doesn't mean you are doing something against the will of God.

128. Bible Dictionary, "Apostle."

129. Reynolds, Daniel/Sermon, Daniel/McKee, Benjamin/Platzman, Daniel, Smoke + Mirrors, Interscope Records and KIDinaKORNER Records (2015).

130. F. Enzio Busche, "Unleashing the Dormant Spirit," BYU Devotional, May 14,1996.

131. "I Need Thee Every Hour," *Hymns* (1985), no. 98.

132. M. Russell Ballard, "Be an Example of the Believers," *Ensign*, Nov. 1991, 95–97.

133. "Count Your Blessings," *Hymns* (1985), no. 241.

134. Charles Dickens, *A Christmas Carol*, chapter 5.

135. "Jesus Christ—Gifts and Expectations," *New Era*, May 1975.

136. "Repentance: A Mighty Change of Heart," Brent W. Webb, BYU Devotional (May 18, 1999).

137. Bruce R. McConkie, "'Thou Shalt Receive Revelation,'" *Ensign*, Nov. 1978, 60.

138. *Teachings of the Prophet Joseph Smith*, compiled by Joseph Fielding Smith (Salt Lake City: Deseret Boom 1976), 149.

139. Brigham Young, *Journal of Discourses* 1:312.

140. Bruce R. McConkie, *A New Witness for the Articles of Faith*, Salt Lake City: Deseret Book Co. (1985), 71.

141. 1 Nephi 8:12 ("And as I partook of the fruit thereof it filled my soul with exceedingly great joy; wherefore, I began to be desirous that my family

should partake of it also; for I knew that it was desirable above all other fruit").

142. F. Enzio Busche, "Unleashing the Dormant Spirit," BYU Devotional (May 14, 1992).

143. Personal missionary journal (January 1, 1995). ("A gift that's given grudgingly is like no gift at all. So if you give to God that way, your blessings will be small. So some just give more willingly to get those blessings, but not me. I have so much more charity. I let God keep his blessings; still I give, but give unwillingly.")

144. Dallin H. Oaks, "The Challenge to Become," *Ensign*, Nov. 2000, 32–34.

145. *History of the Church*, from a discourse given by Joseph Smith on June 9, 1842, in Nauvoo, Illinois; reported by Eliza R. Snow.

146. Thomas S. Monson, "With Hand and Heart," in Conference Report, Oct. 1971 (Adapted from a quotation by Johann Wolfgang von Goethe).

147. Dieter F. Uchtdorf, "The Love of God," *Ensign*, Nov. 2009, 21–24.

148. *How the Grinch Stole Christmas*, Universal Pictures, 2000.

149. Dallin H. Oaks, "Joy and Mercy," *Ensign*, Nov. 1991, 73–75.

150. See also Mosiah 4:3 ("they were filled with joy").

151. David O. McKay, *Pathways to Happiness*, xi.

152. Attributed to Mark Comp Water, *The New Encyclopedia of Christian Quotations* (1995), Hampshire UK: John Hunt Publishing Ltd., 536.

153. David Foster Wallace, *This Is Water*, Commencement Address, Kenyon College (2005).

154. We also can have peace amid adversity. As President Eyring explained, "The disciple who accepts a trial as an invitation to grow and therefore qualify for eternal life can find peace in the midst of the struggle." (Henry B. Eyring, "Adversity," *Ensign*, May 2009, 23–27.)

155. Richard G. Scott, "Finding Joy in Life," *Ensign*, May 1996, 24–26; emphasis added.

156. David A. Bednar, "Therefore They Hushed Their Fears," *Ensign*, May 2015, 46–49.

157. Henry B. Eyring, "Spiritual Preparedness: Start Early and Be Steady," *Ensign*, Nov. 2005, 37–40.

ROBERT REYNOLDS manages multi-platinum recording artists and works in entertainment law. He served a mission in South Carolina before receiving a bachelor's degree in English from Brigham Young University and a JD from New York University Law School, where he was honored with the Jack Katz Memorial Award in Entertainment Law. Robert was an associate in a New York City law firm and now practices law in Las Vegas, where he represents authors, actors, UFC fighters, and various bands and musicians, including the internationally acclaimed Imagine Dragons (whose lead singer, Dan Reynolds, is his younger brother). Robert and his wife, Erica, are the parents of four children.